Words & Flesh

By Carmen Firan

Poetry
Inhabited Words, 2007
Disconsolate Conquests, 2004
In The Most Beautiful Life, 2002
The First Moment after Death, 2001
Accomplished Error, 2000
Punished Candors, 2000
Places for Living Lonely, 1999
Pure Black, 1995
Staircase under the Sea, 1994
Tamer of Stolen Lives, 1984
Paradise for Monday, 1983
Illusions on My Own, 1981

Fiction
The Second Life, 2005
The Farce, 2003
Getting Closer, 2000

Screenplays
Stars' Owner
Dream Trap
A Trio for Inferno
Light in The Attic

Anthologies
*Naming the Nameless: An Anthology of Contemporary American
Poetry* (co-editor), 2006
*Born in Utopia: An Anthology of Modern & Contemporary
Romanian Poetry* (co-editor), 2006

WORDS

&

FLESH

selected fiction and essays

by

CARMEN

FIRAN

with a preface by Andrei Codrescu

Talisman House, Publishers

2008 • Jersey City • NJ

08 09 10 7 6 5 4 3 2 1 FIRST EDITION

Text and titles: Goudy Old Style

Book designed by Samuel Retsov

Cover painting, "At the Beach" (oil), by Constantin Piliuta
Reproduced by permission of Ana Maria Piliuta

Published in the United States of America by
Talisman House, Publishers
P.O. Box 3157
Jersey City, New Jersey 07303-3157

ISBN 10: 1-58498-060-5
ISBN 13: 978-1-58498-060-5

ACKNOWLEDGEMENTS

Many thanks to the translators of my short stories: Mona Nicoara: "Little People" — Dorin Motz: "A Light in the Attic," "The Fur Hat," "Concession," and "Parking" — Doris Sangeorzan: "The Boiler Man" — Julian Semilian: "The Intruder" Many thanks also to Bruce Benderson and Cynthia White Hichens for reviewing some of the English versions.

Special thanks to Alexandra Carides for her continuous support for this book and for transporting my essays "Flesh of Words" into English. My thanks, too, to Maurice Edwards for editing English versions of works included here. All my gratitude goes to Edward Foster for his dedication to my writings and for making possible the publication of this book.

Earlier versions of some of the stories and essays from this book were previously published in the following magazines, collections of prose, and anthologies: *The Brooklyn Rail*, (2006), *Aspasia*, (International Yearbook of Central, Eastern, and Southeastern European Women's and Gender History), *Wreckage of Reason: An Anthology of Contemporary Experimental Prose by Women Writers*, (2008), *The Second Life* (East European Monographs, Boulder, Colorado, 2005), *Lettre Internationale* (Spring, 2007).

CONTENTS

Words & Flesh

Andrei Codrescu

PREFACE: A FAN'S NOTES

In the paper house of words, Carmen Firan occupies a sunlit room. Whenever she goes anywhere, whether in the bazaar of Queens to buy chick-peas from an Egyptian or olive-oil from a Greek, or to the Black Sea to speak before a distinguished audience of Romanian *literati* so steeped in books they give off a babylonian hue, Carmen takes her house of words with her, folded in the shape of a fan. As she banters with her neighbors or exchanges health (physical and mental) information with them, or intones eruditely over the sound of the sea, she fans herself expertly, picking up cadences and phrases that are instantly absorbed into her fan. I imagine that later, when she unfolds her house of words again and sits before the window on which she taps her new discoveries, she becomes many Carmens: Carmen the story-teller, Carmen the poet, Carmen the hypnotist-healer, Carmen the thinker.

In this collection, we meet Carmen the story-teller, a sharp observer, an ironist, an exacting but tender flayer of reality's outer skin. The immigrant plumber and the exiled artists who live between worlds (though they might physically reside in Queens) find themselves at home in Carmen's stories. Her characters move leisurely in these tales, like guests invited to a very special party the purpose of which is known only to their hostess. That purpose, revealed or half-revealed, is that of making them feel OK about being strangers in a strange land because there are no strangers or strange land inside the human body (or else all *is* strange), and, anyway, they are in Carmen's compassionate house of words where wine and talk flow as if no one has ever left the womb. Naturally, they all have to leave sometime (as the wonderful plumber in "The Boiler Man" reflects), and when they do, Carmen the thinker appears, reflecting about the condition of strangeness, of not being home, of being home, of what the word "home" means.

Carmen the thinker meditates on words until she suddenly metamorphoses into Carmen the sorceress, a powerful figure capable of healing and destroying. She chooses to heal and discovers that powerful images can cause physical transformations. Her metaphors put on bodies, her words dress up. Soon, outside her door form several lines: shabbily dressed peasants descending straight down from an immemorial history, immigrants from the twentieth century dressed in second-hand clothes from the pushcarts of lower Manhattan, and an elegant and aloof clientele of monocled esthetes and ivy-covered neo-byzantine elegiasts who do their best to pretend that they are not with the others. Carmen receives them all.

Carmen's sibylline and hypocratic personae are evident in this book of "Flesh and Words," as are her fabulous story-telling gifts. She is simultaneously the Chekhov of Queens and the Sorceress of the Carpathians. Personally, I am lucky to know her also as Carmen, my friend, who knows everyone and everything going on in the world of letters on both sides of our Atlantic (from Sibiu, Transylvania through Bucharest, Romania to Queens, New York and Miami, Florida), and I am fortunate to be able to call on her unfailing sense of what goes on in this world. I get pretty confused most of the time. From a distance (any distance, no matter how far) I can land like an ungainly and muddy octopus right on the exquisite carpets in her sunny house of words, and be welcome. That's a privilege, surely, but she has many friends who feel equally benighted by her generosity.

After all this, to say that she has impeccable taste might sound like a turkey gobbling after the nightingales have sang, but I mean it to mean that she knows true measure, that she is demotic and sound. Her stories and essays, like her poetry, fold perfectly into her instrumental fan. The reporter might say that she knows how to hear and how to render, and the poet that she can find the music in the noise. The rest of me just digs reading her.

FICTION
WORDS OF FLESH

THE BOILER MAN

In buildings like this, boiler men are indispensable. Especially during winter when the radiators clog, filters need to be changed, and pipes crack just when you need them most, on a frosty weekend. The residents at 89-13 were lucky. The super was also a boiler man, a member of a profession learned and practiced diligently in Eastern Europe where everything's out of order or out of place.

Maybe the term "plumber" is more precise, but in his native country his specialty had been radiators. Back during the communist era, the boiler man had an ace up his sleeve since rumors had it that the secret police kept track of suspects by planting microphones in the radiators of suspicious tenants. He had to be trusted — not just skilled — to convince people that he didn't work for the police.

Dick, who had won the green-card lottery, took his wife and daughter by the hand and didn't stop until they reached Sunnyside, Queens. There, in only two weeks, he found this job as a "super" — the guy who does everything.

"I don't believe in lotteries and that stuff about luck. I played on a whim to prove to myself that I couldn't win. Everything I ever got in my life was through hard work. Nothing ever fell into my lap. This time, God knows, the devil stuck his nose into it. I didn't really want to move to America, but once I got the visa, I figured, why not go and see how they live over there." That's what he confessed every chance he could, caressing a bushy moustache he thought boosted his sex appeal. "But I don't like it here. I miss my little house and the vines and fruit trees in the courtyard, I miss my drinking friends and life over there, poor, sure, but happy. I worked, I didn't work, something came up and I lived well, whatever. If it wasn't for my wife, who kept bugging me about my daughter's future and all that stuff, I would never have left everything behind."

Dick looked like he could lift three buildings at once. He wore large denim overalls without a shirt, an outfit that showed off his muscular arms and hairy chest. His "super's office" was in the building's basement, surrounded by boilers, air conditioners, tool, old furniture, torn mattresses, all kinds of useless items, and garbage bags. Basically, Dick ruled an underground empire.

At night, when the garbage was taken out in the well-to-do neighborhoods of Queens, Dick hit the streets in his vintage car, packed it with whatever could be reused, and unloaded his loot in the basement. He managed to stack up a serious collection of TV sets, microwave ovens, tape recorders, chairs, vacuum cleaners, rugs, outdated computers, and whatever else one might need to outfit a brand-new home. Some were in great shape; others he fixed and sold for nothing to newly arrived immigrants who'd ended up in Sunnyside. "I'm doing a good deed," he'd explain defensively, "this is what I learned at home. Take from the rich, and give to the poor. What I get out of it isn't important. It's more of a communal gesture, since everybody here is so into the collective spirit."

Dick had won over all the residents in the building he administered quite competently. He carried old ladies' grocery bags to the elevator, walked dogs, babysat for young families, tended the lawn outside the building, and, of course, replaced pipes and filters, unclogged toilets, and, since this was the country of technology, fixed computers, too. He couldn't really be called industrious, but he was smart, skilled. He never refused a tip but didn't rip anyone off either.

This new world didn't scare him anymore. He'd found out he could get what he wanted even without speaking the language because Sunnyside was populated by his countrymen. The stores, restaurants, pastry shops, medical offices, churches, and newspapers in his native tongue tempered his longing for the mother country. Occasionally the ghetto bothered him, and he'd snap with superiority, "You immigrate to get rid of these folks and end up living with them. It's the same ethnic borsht, only thicker."

Despite rebuffs, he was capable of shedding tears over a native folk song heard in bodegas where people argued for the democratization of the old country, which some denigrated, some regretted, though none would ever admit that they felt like foreigners in both places. It was an unspoken dilemma they would be buried with.

"Well, they have everything here, except tomatoes like the ones back home," Dick sighed over a glass of vodka, which was emptied more and more often and earlier and earlier in the day.

Dick was a romantic. A giant with delicate features, he was sensitive to miniatures. He loved small animals; maybe that's why the mice and bugs that haunted his "super's office" in the basement didn't faze him. He didn't protest the rabbit his daughter brought home, the rabbit which they kept in the bathroom; he loved the flashy fish swimming in an improvised bowl, the jar for pickles that they took out to the balcony in summer. He loved etchings and had even tried to find work as a house painter. With or without his clients' consent, at the end of a job he painted thin stripes and floral motifs that set off the walls from the ceiling, a delicate water lily around the chandelier or colorful birds above the kitchen window.

"We have to embellish our life," was his motto, which he practiced how he knew best.

His large hands, accustomed to pipes and hardware, could be gentle and soothing. He caressed animals, tended flowers, and cried during love scenes. Despite the dirt under his nails, and his T-shirts soaked with sweat at the chest and underarms, he wasn't a repulsive boiler man. You noticed his virility and not his smell, his vigor and not the clothes worn out from crawling underneath sinks and toilets. He loved his wife and adored his daughter, whose every whim he accepted. Provided she was good in school and behaved.

"Life is a simple thing. I don't believe in chance. Everything fits together, and as long as you act with common sense, there are no great surprises. If you can avoid abuse and excess, life is decent, the way it's supposed to be. I'm not an intellectual, but I feel certain things, I don't know how. My grandfather was illiterate, but he knew everything. He died in peace one afternoon, after he'd washed and shaved, called grandmother to his side, held her hand, and told her that his time had come. He closed his eyes and a few minutes later he was gone. Light, beautiful, serene. Now people die with violence, death isn't liberation any more, but a condemnation, a humiliation."

Dick hadn't read one book since graduating from vocational school, a two-year program where he learned all about the heating profession. He only watched movies and sometimes leafed through newspapers. Still, nature had given him poise that could pass as wisdom, perhaps inherited from his grandfather. He had some odd habits too, which could make him an interesting drinking partner.

In the evening, a few friends he'd made in the building descended to the basement, where he had improvised a warm, bar-like atmosphere that resembled his home back home. He'd brought in a plastic garden table from the street and a few odd chairs, even a sun umbrella that he stuck proudly through the hole in the center. Next to it he kept a cooler filled with beer and vodka. He and his companions played folk music and debated the state of the world. One neighbor came from his hometown. They'd been neighbors even back then and left the country just a few months' apart. It's a small world, but even smaller in Queens.

"Guys, I don't know why, but since I left the old country, I've been plagued by memories. I remember everything, you know, everything! Early childhood, my birth, even before it."

The boiler man amazed them with his stories, which included some disturbing details, like remembering his own birth.

"No kidding," Dick would tell them, his eyes blurred by the power of memory. "I witnessed my own birth."

At first they didn't take him too seriously, but in time Dick won them over, and then they listened with baited breath. Each time, they asked him to tell them more stories about being born. They emptied one glass after another, not fully believing what they heard yet moved by such an odd experience.

"Actually I remember details from before I was born, from the time I swam packed in my mother's belly. You don't have much space to move around in there, and your movements are restricted. The last stages of the pregnancy are the worst. Moving gets more and more difficult. You want to turn but can't, you kick with your feet and hands but nothing happens. I remember that during the last weeks I wanted more than anything to do a somersault. A few times I rebelled, I'd grown too much, and I think I kicked my mother too hard because I immediately felt her hands grabbing my heels to calm me down. I recognized her palms instinctively. They caressed me even when I hit her with rage. I wasn't nervous or restless, I had no reason to be, it's warm in there, and you don't lack for anything."

"Didn't you choke?" Dick heard a puzzled voice.

"How could you choke?! I never breathed with more ease in my life. Everything's natural and clean; you wish you breathed air like that all the time! The temperature is constant, same with the humidity, everything's constant, you know what I mean? Just the way it has to be, just as much as it should be. Nothing unpredictable or uncomfortable. You're always satisfied. You're never hungry or thirsty, and if you need food all you have to do is think about it and you're immediately fed with delicacies. You want fish, you can be sure that soon your mother will crave just that, and, because a pregnant woman is always granted her wish, she'll get fish, and you'll extract its very essence, the reason you want to eat fish in the first place. And even if she doesn't eat fish when you crave it, you end up eating the essence of fish, because you extract from her whatever the fish contains. Get it? I'm trying to make everything simple, but I'd like you to understand how it works. You suck in everything you need from her and the poor mother knows it. She loses iron, even calcium. Some even lose their hair or teeth, their nails turn white, their faces have spots and they're always worn out. Whoever says that a pregnancy invigorates a woman doesn't know what they're talking about. It drains her, but you couldn't live better anywhere else. In there I was happy. After I got out, I never felt as protected. It's a divine harmony that's hard to define because we never experience it in real life. My friends, we are born happy. Whatever happens afterwards, God knows!"

Sometimes he'd be paged for an emergency. A flood, a pipe, an anxious old woman whose vacuum cleaner wasn't working. Dick would run there right away, fix whatever needed to be fixed, and come back to the basement where his friends waited for him, enveloped in cigar smoke. He came back with hands even dirtier, sweat dripping down his forehead. He'd curse, gulp a glass of vodka that would ruffle his moustache, knock his fist against the table, and continue his stories.

"What bothered me there, though, was that I had to keep my eyes closed. Strangely enough, I could still see. I don't know what it feels like to be in other women's bellies, but in my mother's womb I saw an extraordinary world. But I never felt any smell or saw any color. Unfortunately I don't know anybody who can confirm my impressions or exchange opinions. I haven't met anybody who was aware of his fetal life or who witnessed his birth. I have a memory, some say, ancient, abnormally large and old. It's possible. And since I moved to Queens it expands every day. Although I believe that memory is infinite. But people don't try to remember that far back, or maybe they can't imagine that it's possible to remember the time before your birth, not to mention the birth itself, which seems so natural, since everyone was present at one's birth, right? If you remember yourself when you were five, why not remember the five seconds after you came into this world? Isn't that the same? The same life?"

His drinking friends would nod in agreement. For the moment, the boiler man's point of view made perfect sense.

"I saw many things in my life, but nothing could top the world in my mother's belly. Entire cities, archipelagoes made of jelly tubes, galleries of pipes stretching like nerves along fluid walls, a complicated architecture of channels, mazes, tunnels and grottos, abysses, a sky of stars, perfect shapes swimming through a delicate spider web, everything murky, like a half-done drawing, like a miniature map of the universe. I could hear my heart beating in the middle of the universe, and I kept floating like an astronaut caught in those transparent laces enveloping me, while rocking me gently like a mild summer breeze. Even stranger, I recognized all these as if I'd seen them before, I behaved as if I had been in my mother's belly before, as if I had memories from another pregnancy. I wonder if I was born more than once."

At this point his audience usually lost patience. Some mumbled in protest that they were being dragged into surreal territory, others looked at Dick with pity, a grown up man, a giant, raving and ranting, but they were all curious to hear the conclusion. Then Dick swallowed another glass of vodka, wiped his moustache with the back of a hand covered with brownish creases, and lowered his voice, while his eyes sparkled conspiratorially.

"There's no pleasure in being born. First of all, it's a long, painful, dangerous process. You pass from that perfect harmony to an unimaginable convulsion, you struggle, you push with your head first, you kick your legs, desperate to get out, nobody knows why, because it was so cozy in there! But at some point you're not allowed to stay inside any longer, you have to leave! The worst is that you feel your own mother straining against you, as if she wanted to get rid of you. At first you lose your balance, you slip, and no matter how much you wrestle, the head drags you down, it suddenly becomes very heavy, as if filled with lead, your ears pop and stress increases. Your head enters a dark tunnel. This is the most difficult and frightening part of the process. The tunnel of darkness."

"I've heard that story about the tunnel before," one of the neighbors told Dick, "but it happens when you die, not when..." He didn't dare say more. The word *birth* had already sent shivers down his spine.

"When you die, it's a tunnel of light," another interrupted, "and in this one it's dark."

"Pitch dark," Dick confirmed. "The first sensation is terrible. You choke, you drown, your hair gets caught in all kinds of roots, and I heard something rumbling like a volcano ready to erupt. I pushed as hard as I could, my neck was stiff, and I thought I'd be trapped inside forever. One of my shoulders was stiff from all that effort. I suffered from pains in my left shoulder until I was five because of my passage through that thin, black, cold, damp tunnel. Then I felt the first smells, just as unpleasant as the sounds that were waiting for me once I was pulled outside. Because the truth is that you can't make it by yourself, eventually you are pulled outside by others. I coughed and I began to sob. They grabbed me, wiped me dry of the lava, and undid the roots wrapped around me, irritating my skin. I was dying of cold, and I'd turned green from all the effort and shouting. I opened my eyes but saw nothing. I heard strange, metallic, piercing screams around me. Suddenly, I felt hungry but this time nothing satisfied me. I'd be administered hundreds of gallons of milk until I was fed up with it. They wrapped me, covered me, and laid me on a bed. I was alone. In my mother's belly I'd also been alone, but here, outside, it was a different way of being alone. Dry. Cold. Deafening. I had only known happy loneliness until then. Now a desperate loneliness began, and I think that's when I was scared for the first time. I understood what it means to be alone. To waver between happiness and despair. To be expelled from the world. To see, to hear, to feel, and not to be understood."

The neighbors were already sad; they drank and experienced

everything as if they'd just been born themselves.

"Look, I remember the first night of loneliness as if it were now. They put me on a bed face up. From there, through the dark window, I saw the moon for the first time. You will ask me how I knew it was the moon. I knew. I'd seen it before. Here, how? Hell knows! And, all of a sudden..."

Dick's phone rang violently. Mrs. Simpson from the 9th floor had an emergency. Her toilet was clogged, and she had guests in half an hour. The boiler man got up at once, duty came before everything else. He left his audience with the story unfinished, grabbed his toolbox, and a few minutes later knocked on Mrs. Simpson's door. She was waiting for him eagerly.

"Dick, you're a miracle. What would I do without you?! God sent you to us!"

LIGHT IN THE ATTIC

Gina wasn't a woman to be easily discouraged. Still, that sweltering afternoon it all seemed more than she could handle. It was unacceptable. Unbearable. Like the melting asphalt into which the heels of her shoes — these days not as narrow as they once were — that sank into the asphalt with a muffled squish. Like the stench wafting from the open doors of the stores. Spoiled delicatessen, rotten fish. Sweaty bodies streaming along the street and bug-eyed girls on the look-out for the nearest subway entrance. Stalls blanketed with watches, belts, sunglasses, postcards with aerial views of Manhattan, overcrowding the already crowded sidewalks teeming with insane passers-by.

She gripped the book tighter under her arm, gritted her teeth, and fingered her handbag, where she had carefully placed the money. The book was merely a cover. She hadn't taken it along to read but to distract people's attention from the handbag crammed with one-hundred dollar bills. No one would dream of attacking an old lady like her, walking peacefully with a book under her arm. No one would discern what the respectful and distracted lady was hiding in her scuffed handbag. Only her expensive sunglasses might, perhaps, give her away. But in a sea of imitations, they might easily pass for an ordinary five-dollar pair such as those that could be found on every street vendor's stand.

The entire street reeked of tobacco, a clear indication that it was already time for the work force to go home. Gina shielded herself the best she could, waving a hand in front of her nose to fan it, grimacing with a barely suppressed disgust. She was choking. In the clammy humidity and the oppressive heat, smoke seemed to coagulate in the air, floating like murderous dark clouds. Disgusting. Detestable. She scanned the street for a cab but found none before reaching the entrance to the subway. As a rule she avoided the subway, primarily out of respect for her former lifestyle when she had a chauffeured limousine.

What she was doing on that particular day, in that area downtown, was another story. Silently she cursed the moment she had decided to take the train into Manhattan, to bail out Mircea once more, Mircea with his damn talent. What a loser! A millstone around her neck!

In the more than twenty years they'd been married, he hadn't accomplished much of anything. Not made one penny or had an exhibition of his paintings. What's more, he hadn't even learned proper English. Well, she had wanted an artist for a husband, now she had one. And now she had to keep him as if he were a disobedient child with his head full of nonsense, spouting stuff like, "the closer you get to the horizon, the farther away it gets from you" or "the rarified yellow light, like a morning of honey" or "the underneath of things, inner states, sensations, representations." All of it nonsense. A painting, you either sell or you don't. But for a long time now he hadn't been painted anything anyone would want to buy.

At least when she met him he was painting flowers, still lifes with fish, women — a bit abstract, but women nonetheless. His work was promising. He had shows, he sold a lot. Now he'd gone off. Definitely off. He experiments with all sorts of who knows what, tears it if he doesn't like it. And he doesn't like almost all of it. He reads like a crazy man, paints like a madman, and can't wait to be alone. What the devil is he doing when he is by himself? Collages, stupid modern stuff no one understands! Half of what he produces he destroys, the rest he stores up in his attic, wherever he can fit it, and hardly any room was left now to drop a needle, in this attic big as a church. No doubt he'd lost his marbles.

In the past, she was the one who brought home some customers who would sometimes buy a painting or two. Once a gallery owner bought the entire set of wild flower paintings. This was right after they had moved from Romania to West Orange, New Jersey, full of hope, imagining Mircea becoming famous in New York, and rich, too! Yet another stupid mistake. Why leave Bucharest, where Mircea was at least somebody? What stupidity to abandon their old home with high ceilings, surrounded by grape vines for a plywood shack of a house in New Jersey?

They had met at the opening of one of his exhibits of oil paintings. She had been married before. Her first husband — much older than she — managed to escape the communist regime and immigrate to Paris where he made good money and died, leaving her a tidy sum and precious jewelry in a Swiss Bank. One day a miracle occurred, Mircea was invited to have a show in New York; both got their visas, Mircea took his paintings, Gina her jewelries, and after the show they decided to stay.

She and Mircea could have been a happy couple, he the talented one, she the rich, he the artist, she the shrewd one with her feet firmly on the ground. She had learned quite a few things from her former husband, an antiques collector from an old Armenian family, with a nose for business. "A duo, with her on the drums and me on the violin. You can imagine the sound," Mircea noted whenever the subject of their marriage comes up.

Why doesn't he just keep his mouth shut, what would he be without her? He wouldn't have survived one day without her in America. "She's too tied down to the real world," he cried. "She sees nothing but what's in front of her eyes; never the light beyond the horizon, never the North Star."

That damn horizon, with its shining line! And now what? Who in his right mind would have gone out on such a scorching day, ride the train into Penn Station, then from there board the subway, get off and start walking along those slimy, stinking little streets all the way to Chinatown, to get to that old jeweler's store? In the past ten years Gina had been gradually selling off all her diamond broaches, ruby earrings, and pearl and emerald pendants. And today she had parted with her engagement ring, which her first husband had custom-ordered from Paris. These few thousand dollars would cover their needs for another three or four months. So many sacrifices for a man! As for Mircea, he couldn't give a damn.

She found him in the neglected, weed covered garden behind the house. He was stretched out on the chaise lounge on the shore of the artificial lake, reading with a wide-brimmed hat low on his forehead.

"Mircea! Mircea!" Gina called out to him, impatient and nervous.

Her damp clothes had stuck to her body. Sweaty shoes widened were slipping off her feet. She was out of breath and panting, her face was tense and her lips purple from the effort, she looked like someone struggling with life itself. And with Mircea too, who was always fond of tricks and ironic pranks, flaunting a sense of humor that aging, illnesses, and failures had not been able to blunt.

"Mircea! You deaf fossil!"

The straw hat did not budge. Maybe he had fallen asleep with the book on his chest. Still, he was quite deaf, had been so from about the age of fourteen. In those days he swam in competitions and jumped on the trampoline. "I once jumped so high, my eardrums popped and I lost my hearing completely in the left ear. When they drafted me into the army, they assigned me to telephone duty. In communications, can you believe it? We were once conducting war games. I was sitting in the trenches, with the headphones over my ears. Whenever I heard, *Target number so and so*, I was supposed to pull a lever, after which a soldier was sent outside, who would then fire the cannon, the machine gun, or whatever weapon was called for. The trenches were just a bunch of large holes filled with mud. I was just waiting there, numb with cold, to hear *Target number 3!* at which I was supposed to pull the lever, and so on. And suddenly I saw in the trench a thin little green lizard, with delicate features, like a piece of jewelry. And onto that green fell a stunningly beautiful ray of sunshine. I was watching her, entranced. Apparently, in my headphones, call after call had come and gone, unanswered — *Target number four, Target number five, Target number six!* and so on. Well, not only was I deaf, but now also completely under the spell of this enchanting little creature. So, naturally, I heard nothing, and gave no response. I merely stood there rooted, watching the delicate being for a long time, thus compromising their war games, sowing confusion among the armies and their enemies."

"Mircea! You deaf idiot!" Gina heard herself say as the stood next to the chaise lounge lying in the shade. "What *are* you doing? Sleeping? Aren't you ever going to wake up? You are driving me crazy, you know! I could be assaulted!"

Mircea opened one eye and looked her up and down with barely suppressed amusement.

"Assaulted? But who's the fool to try to rape you?"

"I'm not talking about rape! I could be attacked. Did you forget I had nine thousand dollars with me?"

"Why in the world are you carrying so much money with you?"

"Because you are not able to make any yourself! I sold the diamond ring, that's why!"

"That's a good girl."

"Is that all you have to say? After all I've done for you! Perhaps I deserve a different lot in life. Have you ever stopped to think about that?"

"You're doing the thinking for the both of us!"

"Stop it! Oh, I'm wasting my breath on you. I might have died of fright for all you care. Or of heat! This city has become unbearable."

"OK, OK, calm down. Why don't you go and make some lemonade! And bring me a glass too."

"How about if *you* go and make the lemonade and bring *me* a glass."

"I don't like that lemonade. Brian is not feeling well. He hasn't stepped outside all day."

"I don't know about that, but for a week now he hasn't taken out the garbage, hasn't done any repairs around the house. And look at this mess of a lawn! As for the fence, it's in such bad need of repair that it won't be long before it falls down on us. I seem to have a special knack for surrounding myself with loafers and free loaders. I'm going to take a shower and then lie down for a while. I'm exhausted and depressed. I feel used and ridiculously generous. It seems I can't expect even as much as a kind word, let alone a bit of genuine gratitude or tenderness from anyone around here. I am a fool. If you want to eat tonight, you'd better do your own cooking. Brian can do his usual potatoes with dill, provided he cleans up after himself."

Mircea had stopped listening. He pulled his hat back over his forehead and was now thinking of how much time he had wasted in his life talking on and on for hours with all kinds of poets, artists and other assorted alcoholics or drug addicts, reeking of talent and decadence. They would write their poetry on napkins, do their drawings on tablecloths, and vomit and urinate wherever they could. Some died of cirrhosis, others overdosed, a few had heart attacks. They left behind a very thin, but brilliant, volume of work. Or perhaps he had not wasted his time. That's how things were meant to be. Great things sprang from those meetings of theirs! Sparkling ideas, O, what a lot of ideas!

He heard Brian bustling about in the garden cabin in which he had been living for over ten years. It all started when Gina had the idea of giving a party, not so much to celebrate Mircea's fiftieth birthday, as to mark the purchase of ten paintings by a Soho gallery, a unique event in Mircea's artistic biography. They had invited several New York friends, artists from New Jersey, art critics and journalists from the local papers.

Things had begun to sour between the two of them. They had no relatives in America, no children. And the violin and drum duo sounded progressively discordant, jagged. Gina impatient, Mircea passive. Gina thorough, pragmatic, possessed of social and earthly goals. Mircea airy, absent-minded, dreamy, with his ethereal joys, happy with the light's elasticity, with the vapor of his breath rising each morning when he awoke, thinking only of his easel.

Brian had been brought to that party by a New York photographer, himself a Romanian. He might have been Mircea's age, perhaps a bit over fifty. In the general melee, Brian remained unnoticed, even to his hosts at first. Gina was trying to look busy, conversing gracefully with anyone whose interest she could arouse in an attempt to convince them of the saleable nature of Mircea's work.

Mircea, of course, was patently absent. Gina hoped to enlarge her circle of friends and identify potential buyers for his strange-looking, large-size canvases, which somehow escaped destruction at the hands of their author, who was always unhappy with the way light came through in them or with the apparent lack of the ineffable. Conceits, thought Gina, silly whims, betraying an obvious immaturity. An irresponsible man, driven her crazy under the guise of the unsung, odd artist in search of devil knows what.

That evening Mircea was rather sad. He was bored and irritated with all the bustle and din the guests were making, with his wife's affected smiles and contrived laughs, with the polite conversation and insincere admiration of the guests, who, once they were in your house, and had gobbled up the food and drunk all the alcohol, certainly were not going to tell you they didn't like your artwork! He was sitting in a corner, rather secluded, muttering something unintelligible in a polite but careless tone whenever someone approached to congratulate him. And all along he was getting more and more intoxicated, just looking vacuously at Gina, who was milling about busy and agitated, solemnly overwhelmed by her role as a matron, public relations manager, and impresario.

Brian was sitting in another corner, just as lonely and bored, wondering what he was doing there, why his friend the photographer had insisted that he come with him. He neither knew, nor wished to know, anybody. Later in the evening everyone walked out into the garden. Most of them were already quite inebriated. Gina had planned a barbecue near the artificial lake on the far side of the garden, a place of spectacular beauty that greatly enhanced the market value of the house. She was hauling wine and beer bottles all by herself from the garden house, together with platefuls of hamburgers and assorted meats.

"Get off your butt and do something," she hissed through her teeth to Mircea, while keeping her artificial smile for the benefit of the party.

"I'm sore from hauling all this stuff. I'm practically falling off my legs. After all, this party is for you!"

"For me? All this circus? Have you even asked me whether I wanted it? I can't wait for them all to leave!"

"Why don't you at least try to make some conversation with them?"

"What should I tell them? I can't speak English properly. Besides, I'm deaf."

"You're drunk and, as usual, a pig! In fact you deserve nothing."

"OK, then I'm not going to lift a finger. Did I ask you for anything? All I want is to be left alone, so I can mix me some paints. Have you seen the trees reflected in the lake?"

"May I be of some help, madam?" Brian was heard speaking. Gina started pleasantly and quickly changed her tone. Turning her back on Mircea, she spoke tenderly to Brian, flattered by his gesture.

"O, you are so very kind! If you wish, you can take these bottles. And could you look after the grill? A man is badly needed in this house!" she added ostentatiously, looking furtively out of the corner of her eyes at Mircea, who couldn't hear her anyway.

Brian took over the husband's role in the household. For one evening it was fun. He took care of everything from the drinks to the grill, serving the guests and satisfying their every wish. He had just finished collecting the empty bottles and had dumped the used paper plates in the large plastic bag. Moreover, he had taken the garbage out and placed it at the curb to be picked up the next day. Then he sat down on a chaise lounge looking out over the lake, transfixed, watching the trees, and listening to the buzz of the insects in the darkness imbued with the odor of burned leaves that had descended over the property of this somewhat dysfunctional couple.

Mircea came over and sat down next to him. He had brought a bottle of wine, which he held tightly to his chest, and two glasses. Neither spoke a word, their silence standing out against the distant background of croaking frogs and women laughing elatedly in the early stages of inebriation.

"Looks like a storm is brewing."

"What's that?" Mircea said, turning his head in Brian's direction.

"We're going to have a storm. The birds are flying in circles, with frequent dips and turns, as if someone were shaking them loose from a desk drawer."

"Very well. I hope all those people will leave soon, so we can be by ourselves and drink a glass of wine in peace."

Brian looked at him silently for a moment.

"I like what you are doing."

"What are you saying?"

"I saw some of your paintings. They're good."

26

Mircea was pouring wine into the two glasses. He put the bottle down on the grass and handed a glass to Brian.

"Are you a photographer too?"

"No. I'm not an artist. Actually I quit my job. There comes a time when you just have to stop."

"I see," nodded Mircea in acknowledgement. "I know what you mean, although I've never had a job in my entire life. I am not disciplined. But I do paint, sometimes even as much as ten hours a day. "Then I tear up everything," laughed Mircea. There's very little I like of what I create. I'm just playing. Now I'm toying with some pastel pictures. Rafters and haystacks. Do you know what a haystack is?"

"I do," Brian smiled for the first time in many weeks.

"What kind of job did you have?"

"I worked in a biology lab."

"And what does a biologist do?"

"He researches structures. Tissues. Systems. What's called the inner nature of things."

"I think all crafts and all arts deal with the same issue. The inner structure of things, whatever the devil that might be. I imagine we are made up of an infinity of micro-organisms that fit together into a perfectly functioning whole. A living puzzle. Diversity and coherence. And should one of them take off on a tangent, error occurs. Some call it a virus, others just a disease. All have been in us from the beginning. Health is just a matter of balance. To keep your inner self in harmony lest you stir one of those organisms. But how can we possibly know what we are doing? Do we have in us the necessary control over our inner structure? Are we aware of what's going on in there?"

Mircea refilled their glasses with wine.

"Let's see, now. What methods do we have to get beyond what is seen? Science? Good. She is always doing her job. Studying, searching, decoding, and, especially conquering. Yes, conquering! As a matter of fact, science is warfare. She wants to dominate, to control everything. On the other hand, we have faith. Goood! Something more intricate. Illusory states of spiritual uplifting. We seem to understand, only to sink into the unfathomable. Naturally the Creator was not so careless as to leave us the mystery unprotected. The Creator did his job. He gave us enough. The Word and the Light: *Now, my dear ones, go ahead and do what you will with them. And should one life prove insufficient, I am going to give you a few more, but you still won't get anywhere. Just like these people, with their science, they do what they do, and still end up short.*"

Mircea lifted his glass and drank up. Brian was seemingly no longer listening to him. Yet, when Mircea stopped speaking in order to pour into his glass the last drops in the bottle, Brian looked at him expectantly.

"Well, there's still art. And I think the Creator has a weakness for it. He is sensitive to interpretations."

"Mircea, Mircea! Aren't you coming? Look, the guests are leaving."

"Let them leave!" he whispered to Brian, hiding behind his deafness.

"Mircea!" shouted Gina from the deck.

"Go and tell her I'm soused, and would ruin her image if I showed up like this in front of her precious company. Tell her, too, I just realized I'm fifty and this piece of reality really hit me kind of hard. There's no way any serious man can remain indifferent to such a blow. Fifty years old! And I've got so much still to do!" chuckled Mircea.

Brian stood up to take the message to Gina. He was tall and gaunt, with delicate movements like those of a ballet dancer, melancholy and mysterious.

"And on your way back, can you get us another bottle of wine, please?"

"I think I should also leave."

"To go where?"

"That I really don't know."

"Then stay here."

Gina gave up trying to get Mircea to see the guests off. Anyway, he would have been morose and unpleasant. Better he should stay where he was. Leave him to his own devices, while she kept up appearances.

Brian had returned with another bottle of wine from the refrigerator, strategically placed in the summer cottage. His friend the photographer was waiting at the top of the stairs.

"It's late and Dan is waiting for me."

"Dan?"

"The photographer."

"Ah, Dan! Romanians are talented. They are all over the place now. But I prefer chicken. How about you? I thought you said you didn't know where you would go."

"I don't. I've crashed at Dan's place for the past two months. Now his girl friend is back from Romania, so I have to leave. He said he was going to try to talk to some neighbors of his, who might have a room in the basement."

"Don't leave just yet. Stay a bit longer, so we can drink another glass before you leave. In fact, why don't you stay here, since you've got no place to go to?"

"What do you mean, stay here?"

"You just stay here. You can live in this little cabin. It's not much to speak of, but you've got everything you need in the way of basics. Electricity, heat, a bathroom, and a television set. Plus a refrigerator filled with drinks," said Mircea.

"No... I can't... I haven't told you everything."

"You've told me enough. Shortly after you turn fifty you get the jitters. You've left your job, quit everything, and given yourself over to ideas. Becoming a tramp, some kind of vagabond, as Gina would say. Irresponsible. But I do understand. Life is so short and we do nothing with it. Got any children?"

"Oh, no."

"Very well."

"Family?"

"Look, I really can't stay."

"Nonsense! Come to the attic, and I'll show you what I do."

Mircea led the way, holding the freshly opened wine bottle tightly by the neck. Brian followed in silence. When they passed Gina, Mircea whispered, "Dan can leave, if he wants. Brian will stay."

"Where are you two going?"

"Upstairs, so I can show him my latest work."

"Oh," said Gina, glad that finally he was showing someone his work.

This was a rare occurrence. Usually he wouldn't allow anyone into the attic. And he never even invited her to come up there.

"And stop drinking!"

"Oh, what a nag she is!" Mircea grumbled, climbing the narrow wooden stairway with an effort. "She is stalking my every gesture, even counts my breaths. See, I am gagging now. That's what she's doing to me. I am endowed with infinite patience. Infinite indeed!" lamented Mircea, panting in rhythm with the creaking of the steps.

The attic was spacious, like a church. Near the entrance a gray tomcat and a tabby were rolling playfully in mutual enchantment.

"Samson and Delilah," said Mircea, introducing them. "For them this is a genuine paradise. The attic is full of mice."

The attic was large and jammed with things. It seemed as if the contents of several households had been deposited there helter-shelter in cardboard boxes, trunks, garden utensils, scraped window and door frames, clothing, pots and pans, sports equipment, lumber, plywood, mannequins, and all sorts of odds and ends.

"When we moved in, ten years ago, I couldn't settle in any room. They were clean but small with such low ceilings that I always felt my head would pop through. With floors smelling of chlorine. Gina was dreaming of arranging a studio upstairs for me in the large room where everything would be tidy and civilized and where people could come and admire me while I worked, buy some paintings and study the artist in his own element. The understanding was that I, too, would be clean, organized, and tidy, wearing an apron with just a touch of paint discreetly spread on it, enough to convince the visitors that I *was* painting, but with my hands always white and clean, ready to shake any customer's. Alas, I chose the attic!"

"It's a marvelous place!"

"Sure! Besides, here I can be all by myself. Gina comes up only when she needs to throw something away. Most of the mess you see is her work! She does it all out of spite to colonize my private space!

She shuffles up here into the attic as many as two or three times a day under the pretext of having to stow some old things away but actually simply to check up on me. Am I painting or am I idling? Do I keep the painting or tear it up in the end? Am I drinking? Or perhaps smoking dope? Do I feel at peace with myself? That's what she hates the most: that I can be happy without her. It's the worst kind of offence for her. I know she'll never forgive me for that. But you know, I had to fight for this solitude. It hasn't come cheap."

"I bet it isn't that easy to get," agreed Brian absent-mindedly.

Mircea poured wine into two dirty glasses and handed one to Brian. At that moment the door creaked open and banged against the wooden pillar. Discreetly, Gina stuck her head around, then stepped in triumphantly.

"What are you guys doing here?"

"Having fun and gossiping about you."

"Well, why am I not surprised! I just came to leave these empty beer cartons and bottles."

"Wouldn't it have been easier to put them into the trash?"

"You never know when we might need them. Watch your drinking, Mircea! All the guests have left."

"Very well!"

"Your conduct was abysmal. Still, it was a good party, wasn't it?" she said to Brian. "By the way, thank you for all your help. Has he shown you his paintings?" she said but did not wait for his answer, shuffling her slippers down the wooden stairs.

"See how diabolical women can be? They are bent on keeping us under their thumbs, pestering us to no end, pounding us into fine powder like termites until there's hardly anything left of us!"

"I'm hardly qualified to offer an opinion on this."

"This obsession with hoarding everything is almost like a disease. She simply can't part with anything, collecting whatever comes her way, restoring and neatly organizing everything. Her need to possess goes far beyond the range of the useful. In fact, I bet she includes me in that special category she reserves for useless things."

"Mircea, don't forget to switch the light off when you leave," shouted Gina from the bedroom door.

Mircea shook his head, hopeless.

"When I first stepped into this attic, I knew it was going to be my very own private place. From that day on, I've never regretted leaving behind our house in Bucharest. No more nostalgia. The attic seemed at first so vast and empty that I hardly knew where to place my easel. But it was full of mice, bees and pigeons. There were droppings everywhere. In the spring I built nests for swallows, and in the fall I laid out baskets with walnuts and peanuts for the squirrels gathering their winter supplies."

He poured himself more wine, studied Brian cautiously, and pulled off the sheet covering a stack of recent canvases.

"I've had quite a bit of success these past few days."

Brian took each of them in his hands, then held them out at a distance, so he could examine them like an expert, tilting or lowering his head, to see them from different angles, under different kinds of light.

"I don't know much about painting," he said at last.

"Thank God."

"But I do like what you do. These things convey something. They are alive. They have a certain mystery about them. They stir up something in me. Certain states, recollections, feelings. I can see beyond them. I am experiencing a kind of joy, I don't quite know

33

how to put it."

"You see, this is precisely Gina's problem. She has no interest whatsoever in finding out what's beyond things. She cannot see further than what the physical eye can see. She lives exclusively on the outside. And that's what's keeping her from being happy!"

"Who *is* happy?" inquired Brian, turning towards him.

"Well, *I* am!" exclaimed Mircea, opening his arms as if he would embrace the entire attic. "Here and now. Every morning when I wake up and I have another day in which I can paint. I stand in this attic before my easel and I'm happy. And the light comes through each day in a different color, with a different brightness, according to the season, to the atmosphere, and to the degree of humidity. It is soft and mild, with orange tones on autumn mornings, reddish, blazing hues just before a storm. There are times though when it is so sharp I could cut myself on it. Or so cold and icy my fingers would freeze on the paint brush. At dusk it is corporeal and heavy, while in early spring it is rarefied and translucent. And at times it is dark, very dark, almost black, preventing me from seeing anything. I have a good relationship with light. I could paint it forever. In the scales of a fish or on a woman's thigh, in the eyes of the monks, on a knife's blade, or in this glass of wine. *Ad infinitum.* I never get bored, can never have enough of it. I only dread the day I won't be able to paint anymore."

"Mircea! Enough! Let's go to bed! Put out the light," Gina called imperiously.

"Pay no attention," Mircea said unperturbed. "Since we have no children, I'm the only one she can order and the sole object of her torture. Otherwise, she's quite a decent girl. I guess each of us is aging according to his or her soul — I in silence, she shouting her lungs out."

By now they had drunk the second and third bottle of wine. Brian continued to study the canvases, as if he were going to buy one but couldn't make up his mind which.

"I like these two haystacks. One green, the other blue; one in the light, the other in the dark. This picture is so sad, so tenderly sad."

"Well, it's a composition — a sensual one. *The complementary pair.*"

Brian started, jerking his head sideways.

"My partner died."

"What's that?" asked Mircea, remembering he was deaf.

"Two months ago my partner died. I quit my job and moved out of my apartment. I just couldn't face living there alone. You have no idea what it's like to lose your matching half. Each morning is a punishment. I wake up defeated. Purposeless. I'm just waiting for the end. Why did I survive him? Where's the blame in this, if there is one? I am too weak to put an end to everything, the way I should."

"Gina must not know this," warned Mircea. "She sees things in black and white. Let this be our little secret."

That evening Brian moved into the summer cottage. The next day Mircea woke earlier than usual, made some coffee, and went to Gina's bedroom.

"What's the matter with you?" she asked, frightened. "Did anything happen?"

"I just wanted to indulge you a little while."

"Have you done something stupid?"

"*Au contraire!*"

"I'm sure you must have made some mistake and now you want to smooth things over before I find out."

"I told Brian he can live for a while in the cabin."

"Whaaat?"

"Calm down. Just think, he can help us with the house, the garden..."

"You mean help *me*! Because you don't lift one finger. You have no idea of the world we live in."

"Precisely. It will make it easier for you. He's willing to do anything."

"So?"

"So that's it! He's going to stay with us."

"What about rent?"

"No rent, but we won't pay him for services either. It's not going to cost us a dime, think about it."

"Well, come to think of it," said Gina, a bit more placated, "we do need a man around this house!"

"See?" chuckled Mircea. "It's going to work out great!"

Ten years had elapsed since the party. Brian became a member of the family, and a daily witness to the cold war fiercely waged between Mircea and Gina. He was constantly called on to come to the defense of one or the other – a convenient safety valve for both of them. He did everything, took care of the house and the garden, too. But most of all, he listened. Both needed to be heard, pitied, encouraged, contradicted and, above all, allowed to speak, to get things off their chests. In a sense, he had become a kind of private shrink, armed with patience, and so quiet and forlorn that he seemed wise and understanding.

They were living in a kind of peculiar triangle. Gina and Mircea could no longer imagine life without Brian. Gina kept selling jewels from the family's heirlooms, in order to cover the household's needs. Mircea went on, passionately painting pictures no one wanted. The monotony was broken occasionally by Mircea's ideas.

"Let's take up bee-keeping."

Brian found himself a protective suit, bought a beekeeper's manual, and installed three beehives in the backyard. For a while everything went well.

"Bees! That's all we need!" protested Gina. "It's like he's competing with himself to invent ways to drive me crazy! I can't even step into the garden these days, with all that humming. Besides, no one eats the damn honey. What a headache!"

In the end the beehives disappeared.

"Let's plant garlic! Lots of garlic! Every fall in the next town they have a garlic festival. We'll win the big prize! The soil is great. Brian, why don't you dig the entire garden?"

Brian dutifully complied.

"Have you gone raving mad? What in the world are we going to do with so much garlic?"

"Well, we'll win the competition and then we'll sell it."

"And where exactly do you plan to sell it?"

"Brian knows! He'll take care of it. I guess at Sunday's farmer market. Didn't you say we should be practical? You're finally getting there! We're making some money."

"Selling garlic? You've got to be kidding!"

"Yes, selling garlic! What's wrong with that?"

"You men have gone insane. And I'm not going along with it."

The following year they harvested an impressive crop of garlic. It didn't bring them a prize, nor did they sell any of it. Instead they put it in the attic, where it provided them with an ample supply for years. Evenings, Brian would cook potatoes with dill and garlic — a recipe the family adopted as the specialty of the house.

In time they tried all sorts of things, like opening a boat-repair shop, although only a handful of neighbors had boats on the artificial lake. Then they turned to planting tea, a small vineyard, a pheasant farm, and a silkworm nursery. Each of these enterprises lasted about a season, until Mircea came up with another idea, only to see it fail, like the others. Brian fulfilled his whims, worked hard and abandoned each project as quickly as he had taken it up. Gina had grown accustomed to the insanity of the two men and eventually stopped protesting.

Mircea spent his time in the attic, painting. Always grumbling about the outcome, but nevertheless happy. Only Brian was admitted into the attic. Mircea would call him up on the pretense that Brian needed to sweep the place clean or that he wanted to show him his paintings. Inevitably, each visit would lead to long conversations that would end by stirring Gina's jealousy. He never ripped up any painting Brian liked. In the evening they would leisurely drink wine out in the garden into the late hours of the night.

Most of the time Brian was quiet and resigned. Often he caught a cold and didn't get better quickly.

"Have you thought of getting some kind of treatment?"

"What's the use? My partner followed a treatment. A useless agony. Brought him no relief. The end is always the same. Besides, I have no desire to go on."

"What?!" Mircea burst out. "Life is a miracle! I would get myself several if I could. What about this honey autumn light or the scent of these crushed grapes, what about the chirp of the crickets, the rustle of the wind, the sky before the storm? Don't you like it here, with us? Why don't you try some medical help? You know, wonders never cease! There are miracles!"

Brian was silent. When he did speak, his voice shook gently.

"I like living with you two."

He spent mornings with Gina, helping her clean house, do the shopping, wash the dishes, take out the garbage; then he'd resume his garden work, which seemed endless. In the afternoons Gina brought her chaise lounge into the garden, and Brian sat on a low stool next to her, massaging the soles of her feet. Gina would then launch into memories about how happy she had been living with her former husband. She had been spoiled rotten! Now she was paying for it, she would add. Both literally and figuratively.

"What would I do without you?" Gina would tell Brian. "All by myself, day in, day out! He doesn't even care to show me what he does. Never invites me up there to inquire whether I like his work or to let him know what I think of it — you know, just to chat with me. He thinks I don't understand. He deliberately forgets I was married to an art dealer that I traveled round the world with him. All I'm good for now is to come up with money. What kind of a life is this?"

"But, you know, he *does* care! He appreciates your opinions. It's just that he won't admit it, hates to show he pays attention to you."

"You think so?"

"Definitely. He loves you very much!"

"But why won't he organize a show?" said Gina, to change the

39

tone of the conversation.

"I don't think he has any interest in that."

"We live a quarter of an hour's drive from Manhattan at the beginning of the twenty-first century, and yet one might say we live outside time, cut off from society, avoiding the world."

"And what's wrong with that?"

"I don't know. It's strange. Do you think Mircea is a failure?"

"Oh, no! He's wonderful."

"You know something? He's never dedicated any painting to me. You know what I mean? He's never painted one especially for me. All artists do paintings of their wives. Instead, he doodles on his canvass, his rafters, his haystacks, his monks with those ridiculously distorted faces, and rotten fish. And now he's got another mania: collages! Have you seen some of the stupid stuff he's been painting lately?"

"I like it. There's so much force emanating from his works! So much joy! The way he applies color, the intricate forms he comes up with! With him, everything is imagination."

"I see," Gina nodded, unconvinced. "Everything happens in that mind of his. No connection with the real world."

"And what's wrong with that?" asked Brian, in Mircea's defense. "Reality only brings unhappiness."

"I don't know where you come up with such ideas. You don't mean to tell me you're unhappy. But why am I asking? As though I were any different..."

"No, with you two I'm OK," Brian would whisper as he continued to massage Gina's feet until she dozed off in her chaise lounge with her chin resting on her chest, her mouth barely open.

One afternoon, Mircea came down from the attic earlier than

usual. Brian was fixing something on the lakeshore. Gina had gone to the bank.

"Brian, get your old self over here. We got some work to do."

Mircea's eyes glimmered with barely suppressed anticipation. Brian walked over, slowly, coughing hoarsely, nursing a three-week-old cold.

"I've got an idea. We're going to fly!"

"Fly?" questioned Brian, as if the only unusual thing was choosing to do it right then

"I've just found out how to fly. I wonder why I hadn't thought of it earlier! It's so easy! You'll see."

"How did you find out?"

"It just came to me. It popped into my head," chuckled Mircea. "Everything's up there! All we can ever invent is in our heads."

"So how do you do it — flying, I mean?"

"Piece of cake. You bend down, stretch out your hands and rest on your knees, as if you were a bird."

Brian did as he was told, kneeling down, with his arms wide open and his head bent down. His feet sank into the tall grass. Little swallows were circling noisily above their heads.

"Yes, yes, like that. Keep it up like that. Now, I'm going to sit here next to you. Tense your legs and lower yourself a bit more. And concentrate. That's all it takes: concentration."

Mircea stretched out over Brian's back, his arms resting on his. Then he closed his eyes and held his breath. There they were, like a group statue, caught in a graceful movement.

"There we go! We're flying! Can't you feel we're floating in the air?"

Brian nodded in acknowledgement and followed Mircea's example, closing his eyes. He barely felt the artist's weight pressing down on him.

"Flying does wonders for one's bones. In fact, it's good for every part in the body. So therapeutic! Every flying creature is healthy. Brian, can you feel we are flying?"

"Yes I can."

"Then you are going to get well. What can you see?"

Brian closed his eyelids tighter.

"Blue fields."

"Tell me more."

"A light from above is coming down on my eyes. I can see it. Bright and pure. I can even feel it. "

"Is that so?"

"Vast green spaces."

"Good, good! What else?"

"The tree tops. And the golden grass."

"Can you see the ocean, too?"

"Yes, I can see the ocean."

"Then you'll be healed, Brian. Miracles do happen. Look, right now we're taking part in a miracle. We are causing it to happen. Think hard and tell yourself under your breath that you are going to get well."

They had been flying peacefully for a few minutes when Gina paused in the middle of the garden, looking at them perplexed.

"What the hell are you doing there?"

Her strident voice startled them, and Mircea slid off Brian's back.

"If I told you, you wouldn't believe it."

"Nor would you believe if I told you that I put myself through all sorts of hoops to pay all our bills for the month," retorted Gina.

"What did you say?" asked Mircea, cupping his hand behind his ear.

"That I'm tired of all your stupid behavior. At least you should have the decency not to involve Brian."

"Sorry, I can't hear you."

"And I wish I couldn't see you!"

"We are flying! Would you like us to teach you how to fly, too?"

"Stupid old fool!" snorted Gina and stormed out of the garden.

They would fly several times a week with Mircea lying on Brian's back. And while they were in flight, they told each other what they saw.

Gina would make the sign of the cross, disgusted. How ridiculous men can get! "It's all because you have no job, not a care in the world! However, if you were forced to earn your own living, you would hardly find time for all your goofy ideas."

"You don't know what you're missing in life just because you refuse to use your imagination," replied Mircea sadly. "So many things you'll never feel, never see, and never touch!"

"Sometimes I wonder if you are just a clown, or a real crackpot!"

Mircea was now dividing his time between the attic and the flying sessions with Brian. In the evening they would drink wine by the lakeshore, braving Gina's nagging. They would get drunk and go to bed peacefully.

Except that Brian was getting more and more fragile as the days wore on. He tired easily, coughed constantly, and lost weight, and his eyes had retreated deep onto their sockets. He slept late, collapsed whenever he exerted himself. The garden was overgrown with weeds. Gina grumbled, discontented, while Mircea defended Brian, attempting to conceal his own concern.

On that hot August day, Mircea had had a premonition. Gina had gone to Manhattan in an attempt to sell another of her famous rings to assure their survival. It was past noon, and Brian had still not shown up in the attic. Several times Mircea came down under various pretexts, searching for him in the house and out in the garden. He was nowhere to be found. He pulled the chaise lounge over to the lakeshore, covered his head with his large straw hat, and started reading a book, while watching to see Brian should he show up. It was already quite late.

Gina returned, agitated, having been robbed in plain daylight in Chinatown. She was edgy and exhausted with frayed nerves, showing all the wear and tear her martyr-like existence with Mircea had caused. She went straight upstairs to take a shower and lie down for a while. In the meantime, Mircea grew more alarmed. At one point he stood up, walked to the summer cottage, and put his ear against the door. He couldn't hear a sound. He walked in. Brian was lying on his back with his gentle eyes fixed on the ceiling.

"I thought you were asleep, said Mircea cheerfully, but you are only meditating. What do you want to do? Shall we fly for a bit?"

"I can't."

"What's wrong?"

"Nothing. I just can't do it anymore."

"Come, we're going to switch places. Now you will fly lying on my back. It's going to do you good."

"It won't matter anymore. I don't think I'll be able to fly again."

"OK, OK, just rest for a while," said Mircea, his voice shaking. "Not to worry. We'll fly tomorrow. Why don't you come up to the

44

attic with me, so I can show you my latest paintings?"

"I can't move," whispered Brian.

"All right. You lie still. I'll be back in a bit."

He crossed the garden with long strides, climbed the steps to the attic two at a time, as in his youth, and returned quickly to the cabin, carrying a canvas he had painted that morning.

"What do you say, kid?"

He set the canvas in front of Brian, so he could see it without having to turn his head.

"It's Gina. She's so beautiful!"

"I thought of you, while I painted it."

"And you did a very good job handling the light over her face. She is exactly as she would like you to see her."

"But please don't tell her. She shouldn't know about it. Let's just keep this between us."

"Sure, it'll be our secret."

"I'm scared, Brian."

"I know. I'm too."

"That's why I've painted Gina. I'm scared to be alone. Loneliness is different than solitude. You choose your solitude. To be creative, to put order in your thoughts. It's an energetic state of mind. These days I was thinking of the three of us. Our wonderful sad group. My painting is not enough. I need both of you. Don't go, Brian."

Brian cast him a grateful look. Mircea's hands were shaking. He put down the canvas and rested it against a chair beside Brian's bed.

"Should you change your mind, we can still go for a short flying session. You'll find me by the lake."

He left Brian's cottage exhausted. The sky was overcast. The swallows flew in low circles. They would dive, almost touching the treetops — a sign of the storm's approach as Brian had once told him. He sat down in his armchair and felt helpless for the first time in his life. The laurel bushes were writhing in the strong gusts stirred by the storm. Two years ago he had thought about planting laurel and oleander shrubs. Brian had gone along with the idea. The oleanders froze when winter came, but the laurels adapted themselves to the climate, growing into metallic-green tall bushes. Brian got to like them too. Sometimes he would add laurel leaves to his potatoes. The first raindrops stung his skin.

"What are you doing there?" Gina's voice boomed from the window. "Can't you see it's raining?"

"What did you say?"

"It's raining!"

Gina came down to the garden to pick up the wicker chairs and the chaise lounge before the rain came down hard.

"OK, I understand you can't hear, but can't you feel either? No wonder you can't feel the rain, after smoking another joint. Your eyes give you away"

"The storm is coming."

"Then get into the house!"

"Brian is not feeling well."

"You told me already. I can see for myself how weak he's been lately. What's ailing him?"

Mircea touched her arm and looked at her dejectedly.

"He's going to die."

"What?"

"Brian is going to die."

"Cut it out!"

"It's true."

"Look, I've had enough of your dumb jokes."

"I've always been afraid of this day. It's been our own little secret, his and mine. Ever since that night when he first stepped foot in our house. He didn't want you to know."

Gina surveyed him with a mixture of doubt and terror.

"What do you mean he'll die? What of? I'm going to go see him."

She entered without knocking. Brian was sitting on the edge of his bed. He had turned the picture Mircea had painted that morning towards the wall, having expected Gina would visit him.

"You're going to get well. I promise you." She was speaking in a slow, measured voice, quite unlike her typically loud and fast speech. "We'll go to the best doctor. I know you don't have insurance or money, but don't worry. I'll pay for everything. I've still got two rings that Mircea doesn't know about. They'll fetch the best price by far. Then we'll find the best hospital, the best doctor. No matter the cost, I'll pay for everything."

Brian was smiling as if to reassure her.

"Why didn't you tell me? You've got to get well! How could we ever live without you?"

Brian was no longer saying anything. Not a word. He tried to stand up and Gina helped him. Both of them went out to the garden, Brian leaning on Gina's arm. Mircea was waiting for them. Outside it was pouring firm, hot raindrops. All three looked at each other, as if they had a hard time finding themselves in the midst of an infernally crowded space.

Mircea bent his knees, lowered himself and spread out his arms. Gina helped Brian lie on Mircea's back. Both were holding their eyes closed, while Mircea's palms held tightly to Brian's palms as if afraid they would really lift off the ground. They were flying in silence with Gina beside them. The raindrops were streaming down their cheeks.

"Can you see the treetops?"

Brian nodded as his face was lit by his customary gentle smile.

"Then everything is all right. And the ocean? Can you see the ocean? Beyond it, over there, there's another ocean. And so on, kid, *ad infinitum*. Land, water, light, water, land...."

The rain turned into a thunderstorm. Big flashes of lightning opened the sky. Gina watched tenderly as they flew. She was almost flying with them. She too could see the expanses of blue water, the treetops, the grass in flames, the gloomy light shoot down to earth. She looked at Mircea and understood all his joys and fears. Her man was crying with Brian on his back. She was able to see the line of the horizon ever brighter disappearing with both of them into the sky.

After a week Gina went into the cottage to clean it up. She found the painting, resting against the chair, facing the wall. She stared at it, recognized herself and her heart flooded with tenderness. Except that in the corner of her mouth Mircea had painted Brian's smile. She carried the picture to her bedroom and hung it on the wall facing the bed. She stepped out onto the landing towards the attic, and called, "Mircea!"

No one answered.

"Mircea! Mir-cea! You deaf lout!"

"Come on up! Let me show you what I've been painting today."

THE INTRUDER

The devastating news reached the office of the Minister of Foreign Affairs on Tuesday at 4pm. An ill-fated day for the entire diplomatic corps. Tuesdays are doomed, but this was also the 13th, that unlucky number, a dog-day afternoon that overwhelmed the city with heat, drained its inhabitants of energy, melted the asphalt, maddened the dogs, and roasted basements, causing thousands of rats to throng into the streets.

For the last few years, the weather in the capital of this Eastern European country had gone haywire. At least since the collapse of the communist regime, said the superstitious old ladies as they counted their minuscule pensions in front of shop windows over-stocked with expensive imported goods sold at prohibitive prices.

In the Minister's office everything was fine. At the end of the day, two ceiling fans still swirled in the heat over Gloria's desk, where she'd finished arranging her folders. On the corner of the desk, one envelope would be left unopened until the next morning had she not noticed the red stamp on it reading URGENT. She was a model secretary, noticing everything. Nothing escaped her.

Careful not to touch the envelope with her freshly painted fingernails, she opened it with a deft, rapid motion and cautiously drew out the letter. Her nostrils dilated, her chest expanded, and she leaned her head backwards and broke into laughter. She read the letter again, waving her hands in the air to dry her polish, but also to accompany the peals of laughter that shook her voluptuously beautiful body enveloped in a red mini. Oh, the beautiful women of this country!

"Holy Mary, Mother of God!" For Gloria, this was the supreme exclamation. Both giggling and sobbing, she wiped beads of sweat from her neck with the back of her hand. As she was about to knock on the Minister's door to give him the ridiculous letter, three formidable men with dark faces burst into the office. Gloria was not new at her job, and she knew what this meant. Something serious must have occurred. Just her luck: another crisis at the end of the day, ruining her evening. But how can you complain? International problems outweigh personal ones as they explained when she was hired by the Ministry of Foreign Affairs.

Under normal circumstances, each man would begin an obscure, seemingly casual conversations with her. What a hot day! What a beautiful dress! What wonderful coffee those delicate little fingers of hers had made! And only then would they go into the Minister's office. But this time the three of them charged in, shoving the office's upholstered door open and completely ignoring her.

"Gentlemen, you can't break in like that. I have to announce you. What if the Minister is tied up? I need to ask him if he can see you."

"It's urgent!" the three shouted simultaneously.

Gloria glimpsed at the letter, which was still in her hand, and realizing that the three ministers must have received their own copies, burst out laughing under the horrified gaze of the Deputy Minister, the scornful frown of the Chief of Secret Service, and the desperate eyes of the General Director of U.S. Relations.

"Urgent, urgent!" she cried, "I received this URGENT letter, too. You can't imagine how ridiculous it is! Holy Mother of God, what a crazy world!"

"Ms.," said the Deputy Minister, "I don't know what letter you got, but it's imperative we see the Minister immediately."

At that moment the Minister's door opened, revealing him standing with a disinterested air. He was dressed in shorts with a tennis bag slung over his shoulder.

"Gloria, call the chauffeur," he told his secretary.

Then he noticed the frozen faces of his colleagues.

"Have we a problem, gentlemen?!" It was more an exclamation than a question. Being a cordial person with a sense of humor, the Minister was used to treating the desperate cases brought to him by his subordinates, even the most desperate, in a sportsmanlike manner.

"Disaster!" the three shouted.

"OK, OK, c'mon in. Gloria, get your notebook and come in with us."

The three fidgeted, not knowing whether Gloria should be part of the discussion, but the Minister ignored their reaction, opened the door wider and let his secretary pass first, then without much enthusiasm dropped his shoulder bag in a corner and sank into a walnut chair. Dressed as he was in shorts and tennis shoes with a huge painting behind him, you might think his authority might have been compromised. But the three dignitaries trembled at the very thought of breaking the news to him.

"Come on, come on, gentlemen, it's 4 o'clock already!"

The Deputy Minister, an elderly gentleman who had seen much, both during the communist era and after, rubbed his nervous sweaty palms together, and gripped his tie so tightly that it looked as if he were about to strangle himself. The news fell like a guillotine: "A snake penetrated our diplomatic Mission to the U.N. in New York."

The Minister wrinkled his forehead, trying to understand. Gloria broke into muted laughter. The General Director of U.S. Relations, a young man in a foreign suit with western manners, swallowed the gum he'd been chewing.

"A boa. Four meters long."

The Chief of Secret Service dropped his head in shame.

"What?" The Minister hesitated between a grave and an ironic air.

"Our Mission has been penetrated by what?"

Gloria studied his eyes for a reaction, saw his indecision, and smiled innocently, shrugging her shoulders, said, "A snake, you know? I think..."

The Minister shot forward like an arrow. The other three sank deeper into their chairs and drew their necks back into their collars.

"Are you insane?"

"What is even more serious is that the snake has disappeared," whispered the Chief of Secret Service.

"What do you mean, *disappeared? Where* did it disappear?" roared the Minister, lumbering across the room in his sport clothes.

"Inside the Mission building. They can't find it."

"When did you hear about this?"

"Just now," reported the General Director of U.S. Relations.

"When did it happen?"

"A few days ago."

"Why wasn't I told?"

"An attempt was made to solve the problem at the local level."

"Are you aware of what you're saying? Are you aware of the gravity of this? Recall all the diplomats! Beginning with the Ambassador!" the Minister ordered as he nervously genuflected in the middle of the room.

"With your permission," dared the Deputy Minister, overwhelmed by the sensitive situation, "it might not be wise to proceed this way. We could create a diplomatic crisis, a scandal. This is happening in New York, after all."

"Yes, it's New York, that's the problem. Why couldn't this happen in some hellhole in Africa, or a place like that? This is all we need! In the middle of the war on terrorism! Just when our army is getting fighter planes, when our troops are leaving for the hot zones of the world, when the great powers are finally beginning to notice us, care about us, even accept us, WANT us! When we're struggling to win over America and make her our ally, gain her confidence, get our heads out of water, these idiots lose a snake! What kind of diplomats are we sending to represent our country, gentlemen? And the damn security service, what the hell did they *secure*? Why do we pay these imbeciles?! We give them everything they need to make sure nothing gets by. The latest technology, the highest standards. They're wired, connected to the Internet, to the whole universe, the whole u-ni-verse! Armed, instructed, chosen from the best, and they, what do they do? They let an intruder into the goddamn Mission. At the United Nations yet! A snake! I don't believe it! Not only that, but then they lose it without a trace. Have you ever heard of such a thing?" The Minister's voice was getting hoarse. "And what about all my magnificent speeches, all the work I did for a decent image for this country? Gentlemen, I assure you, it's not easy to draw attention to a small country, even when it has, like ours, such gigantic potential. It is not easy. We were about to gain credibility, our voice has been heard from the Middle East to the White House, and look what happens! This is ridiculous! Absurd! Unfair! How can you have any self-esteem, how can you pretend to be a trustworthy partner when the hallways of your Mission in New York are haunted by a...snake?! Keep the press away from this. No leaks! We'll be the laughing stock of the world. Gloria, get the Ambassador on the phone. And how the hell did the snake get into the building? Tomorrow, first thing, call a meeting of our Homeland Security!"

Feverish hours followed. A crisis committee was assembled, and a secret mission with the code name "Post Meridian" was launched, though it had nothing to do with the news that had upset the order and priorities of the Ministry of Foreign Affairs. The Prime Minister was informed, too, but he decided that the President shouldn't be disturbed yet and gave those responsible twenty-four hours to find a solution. What's more, the Prime Minister was composed and emotionless, which most people took to be a form of cynicism.

Originally a journalist and one of the heads of the former communist youth party during the totalitarian regime that had collapsed only a few years before, the Prime Minister was a powerful figure from every point of view. He had been schooled in Western Europe like all the children of communist leaders, spoke four foreign languages perfectly and dabbled in others, loved to travel to exotic places, was a terrific skier and a passionate hunter. His poised reaction to the terrible news was due in part to the fact that he was an animal lover. He'd adopted two stray dogs, and he raised racehorses, chickens, and ostriches on his farm in the country.

The Minister of Foreign Affairs resorted to threats and forceful measures, but the Prime Minister used a different tactic. The next day he assembled young analysts from the Institute for the Investigation of Conflicts, and within the framework of an open discussion, over a cup of Turkish coffee, asked them to come up with a report on the historical event.

"Certainly, gentlemen, you will resort to symbolism and interpretation, to geo-political and socio-political analysis. You'll evaluate the situation, its long-term consequences and international implications. You'll forgive a little pressure here, but I want to bring everything into the light. I want you to prove your value as best as you can, and there's no better opportunity than this event of Borgesian, Marquesian magnitude. And if we think about it, our mythology is full of monsters and dragons. Excavate your collective subconscious, our traditions, our folklore, and our national spirituality."

The young analysts, a bunch of young men with crew cuts and glasses, fragile gestures and an intellectual air, who had been carefully selected by the Prime Minister himself, absorbed his directions solemnly. Their pens were already twitching impatiently in their pockets. One had the beginning of an erection, which faltered when the Prime Minister urged them to prove their "potential." All kept their eyes on the half-smoked cigar that the Prime Minister had put out in the ashtray.

For them this was the crucial moment to prove their mastery as essayists and specialists in delicate conflicts and to advertise their Europeanism and their capacity to analyze in depth the intricate traps of diplomacy and international politics. All would struggle to project a positive image of the Prime Minister who had invested good money and a competitive preparatory program in them, along with great hopes, now that the general elections were approaching.

These genial young men would oppose the frozen mentality of communism with their dynamic thinking, flexibility, imagination, transparency, and modernity, and change the country's image, still unjustly associated with post-communist phantasms of this East European state, swamped in poverty and corruption.

Meanwhile Operation "Post Meridian" unfurled. The Homeland Security Council met the next day in an extraordinary session. Everything would remain confidential, behind closed doors. They had worked out complex protection measures for the members of the diplomatic corps in New York and elaborated various alternatives for capturing the snake through methodologies specific to espionage and anti-terrorism tactics.

Nobody knows how the press got wind of it, but the next morning, newspapers appeared in special editions in which all sorts of scenarios were played out with journalistic brio, building progressively into paroxysms.

The simple headline: "Boa Penetrates the Corridors of Our U.N. Embassy," became, in a mere few days: "Terror in New York."

"Gigantic boa threatens our diplomats."

"Children could be the first victims."

"Sleepless Terror in New York City."

"When will the families in danger be evacuated?"

"Politics and diplomacy in a state of apprehension and fear."

"The nightmare continues."

A few days later, the newspapers were filled with detailed stories about the escaped snake, or, depending on the particular story, the snake that sneaked in, the snake that came in the mail, the snake that infiltrated the diplomatic mission: "The wife of a diplomat was chased by the intruder for over two hours in the basement, where she'd gone to take out the garbage."

"In his office on the 6th floor, the building administrator spotted the snake's head between two bottles of Scotch, recently delivered for a reception in honor of National Heroes' Day."

"The son of a diplomat was evacuated from his room in the middle of the night after a series of bizarre moans and hisses issued from the closet."

"The wife of the Ambassador woke one morning with horrible muscle spasms. It seemed that the intruder had been coiled around her all night long."

In a country so open to conspiracy and supernatural phenomena, new scenarios followed: imperialistic duplicity, Jewish conspiracy, Masonic plot to weaken our country and manipulate us as they wished, a practical joke played by our diplomats in New York to distract attention from their cigarette smuggling.

People forgot about the heat, the economic difficulties, small salaries, and inflation. Everyone had an opinion, a motive, or a solution for the unsolvable situation. TV channels broadcast documentaries about snakes, interviews with boa constrictor tamers, talk shows with specialists. The whole country became experts in boas. Women in particular, because of their inclination for unusual happenings and miracles, informed themselves as much as they could on boas, so they would seem to know all about their practices, in great detail.

Even the President felt it necessary to appear on television to appeal for calm, tolerance, universal harmony, and understanding, imploring all the responsible powers to work together to overcome this difficult moment.

The President, an optimist in his own right, yet again demonstrated his confidence in the nation's institutions, in the loyalty of the diplomatic corps, and declared himself firmly against any violence or provocation, finishing his speech with the slogan that brought him victory in the elections: "Together we will succeed. Hope is on the way! May God help us!"

The only one who remained perplexed was Gloria, who still

wanted to laugh but was unable to understand the dramatic dimensions this piece of news had assumed. Nothing could have helped her predict the national crisis that followed.

In fact, things became far more complicated. The snake, a splendid boa, had been brought into the building by the wife of the ambassador of a South American country who had been invited to a reception on a national holiday. The distinguished lady showed up with her husband and with the snake wrapped around her neck. She had raised it from birth. It was her pride and joy. It had sparkling yellow scales dotted with brownish stains. It curled around its mistress's neck, complementing her long and elegant gown so well that it looked like an extravagant shawl.

The security officers had not tried to stop her. Perhaps they hadn't even noticed that her shawl was actually a snake. In any case, there were no rules regarding snakes in the building.

The whole evening Madame Ambassador ambled through the halls with the snake which everyone admired. She replied patiently to questions and satisfied everyone's curiosity. "How beautiful and well-behaved it is!"

"How old is it?"

"How long?"

"What does it eat?"

At someone's insistence, she removed it from her neck and placed it on the sofa for inspection. How it then disappeared, no one could remember.

When the reception ended, she looked desperately for the snake under the tables, in the hallways, bathrooms, even on the terrace and roof. The alarm was turned on. Security officers panicked. Only Madame Ambassador remained calm, accepting the fact that, for a while, she would have to live without her pet.

She explained that she had lost the snake a few times before, once in the apartment of a friend. "He showed up again after a week. He hid under the wardrobe. It usually happens when he sheds his skin. I know he looks gigantic, but he can squeeze into the smallest places. I'm worried, but I know he'll show up eventually. Call me as soon as he returns, and I'll come and get him."

"Is it dangerous?" asked the officers, their faces disfigured by fright.

"Oh, no, he's the sweetest and the gentlest, he's never attacked anyone."

The campaign — code name "Post Meridian," under the immediate directorship of the Minister of Foreign Affairs, and in close collaboration with the secret services — decided to send several anti-terrorist specialists to New York on the pretext of repairing the ancient plumbing and sanitation, the roof as well. It was a credible ruse because the diplomatic building was in a sorry state. It hadn't been renovated for decades due to lack of funds, as the Minister of Foreign Affairs kept complaining. Certainly the costs to bankroll the snake operation greatly exceeded those required to repair the building, but this was about international security, the circumvention of a diplomatic conflict with the United States, as well as with the country from which the snake had come.

Among the eighteen specialists trained for such missions, there were a few workers who could patch things up a little. And the Minister of Foreign Affairs, who possessed a practical and inventive spirit, came up with the idea of sending a snake tamer from the state circus.

"I loathe this humiliation. Shall we allow ourselves to be terrorized by a reptile? You will return with the skin of this snake. I want it dead or alive!" the minister shouted, plunging into his walnut chair, and contemplating the vulnerability of countries that find themselves at the crossroads of great empires.

In New York the tension reached a critical level. The families of diplomats slept by turns, no one switched the lights off anymore. They avoided being alone in their rooms. They were exhausted, anxious, their senses in constant high alert, always suspicious of sounds or smells that might indicate the presence of the snake, though no one knew what smell or sound to expect from a boa.

They all agreed that the most frightening daily rituals involved showers and toilets. They'd discovered that boas feed on rats, and the basement of the building would be a paradise for it. The basement teemed with rats and mice scurrying along the garbage dumpsters and washing machines. No one went down there anymore. They threw their garbage directly into the street and refused to wash their clothes.

The building entered a kind of quarantine. Diplomatic activities were reduced to a minimum, visitors were prohibited, and security cameras were installed everywhere to watch and monitor every thing. The diplomats cancelled their meetings, went anywhere for fear that something horrible might happen when they were out. New York, Broadway with its shows, the museums, all the attractions for which the world so desperately yearned, left the diplomats cold: the snake monopolized their attention.

The anti-terrorism team arrived in New York on a Saturday afternoon. After a short meeting with the Ambassador, the eighteen specialists spread out through the building, searching everywhere, dismantling sinks, toilets, pipes, walls. The snake tamer followed with a whistle of Indian origin and other tools. The tenants were happy to cooperate. At least they were not left to confront the beast by themselves. The atmosphere grew more relaxed. Soon snake jokes began to spread, propagated by younger diplomats who hadn't lost their sense of humor despite the professional rigor the situation required.

After a few days, the building was in shambles. Demolished walls, disassembled pipes. The two workers didn't manage to piece everything back together or to repair what the anti-terrorist experts took apart, venturing even into the fabled "snake's mouth" in order to fulfill their mission. A television crew was sent to New York in order to broadcast news from the scene. Every news report opened with headlines like "Breaking news: Snake Eggs Found Under Sink on the 10th Floor." There were updates such us "Live from New York. The War on Terror: Chasing the Boa." Charismatic correspondents with frozen smiles promised a balanced and fair coverage of the crisis.

The snake's mistress telephoned one day to find out if her pet had made an appearance. Her husband had come to the end of his mission at the U.N., and they were due to return to their country. Though she was pained by the loss, she consoled herself with her three other boas. She added, however, that if the snake appeared after her departure, it would be her gift to the Ambassador as a sign of friendship between the two countries.

Then evenings became somewhat more entertaining in the building. The workers played folk music, got drunk, and passed out. Little by little, life grew more normal, though everyone was aware that somewhere, in a corner, a snake was watching.

After a month of detailed and exhaustive searching, only two days before the International Security Council met in New York, the building of the U.N. Mission was to host the head of the Parliament, who was arriving with his special advisors and ministers. The team of specialists was just about to abandon the search when, under one of the heating boilers in the basement, someone found the snake's skin.

The entire building celebrated the event with a private cocktail party. The sparkling yellow skin, dotted with tiny brownish stains, was placed in the office of the Ambassador. People lined up to view it, and everyone acknowledged that it possessed an unspeakable splendor spread over the sofa, glimmering with orange reflections. Then it was carefully wrapped, placed in a diplomatic pouch, locked with a secret code, and transported under great secrecy by four anti-terrorist experts, the very best of the "Post Meridian" action team.

The next day, at exactly 4pm, the snakeskin arrived at the office of the Minister of Foreign Affairs. Gloria spread it out on the thick carpet, a gift from the Iranian Prime Minister, at the foot of the sofa where the Chief of the Secret Service sat next to the General Director of U.S. Relations and various other political advisors.

"Well, I can see the skin. But the snake? Where is the snake?" asked the Minister of Foreign Affairs, without taking his eyes from the orange reflections.

"Disappeared without a trace," the defeated Chief of Secret Service replied.

"This means that it's still in the building?"

"I doubt it. Our men searched everywhere. Maybe after it molted, it managed to escape."

"But we can't be sure, can we?" insisted the Minister.

"We can't be sure of anything."

"You sound fatalistic, gentlemen. We cannot be diplomats if we are to be the victims of superstition and fatalism."

Unfortunately, in saying these things the Minister of Foreign Affairs had unwittingly stepped onto a mine field — the territory of the Prime Minister, who was a thinker, a philosopher, and an analyst who couldn't stand failure. Still, when he did encounter failure, his legendary tenacity pushed him to make the most of it by polishing his image to perfection. So this time the Prime Minister exercised his authority and exhibited his qualities as a charismatic leader in a nationally televised symposium.

He called together the young analysts from the Institute for the Investigation of Conflicts who, in the meantime, had fleshed out complicated reports He notified ambassadors, the President, the press, the unions, the regional party organizations, and within the framework of an impressive reception at the Summer Palace, he expounded his theory: "The Transcendence of the Political and Collective Unconscious." It was sublime, though hardly anyone understood what he was talking about.

The most talented of his disciples, full of pride, presented papers and reports about cosmogony and the symbolism of the snake in the history of the national culture, about the battle between the Angel and the Demon, the gap between East and West, the axis of Evil surpassing the European Union, and made allusions to the infiltration of the diplomatic building of a former communist country by an intruder.

In their subtext, the essays could not forgive the failure to capture the symbolic animal, which was always imprudently associated with cunning, perversity, and diplomacy vanquished by its own weapons. The snake would continue to remain for many a constant threat. Its presence, be it imaginary or fictive, would haunt them for many years in the corridors of diplomacy, in unhealthy basements ,or on roofs reeking of heat.

The works created for the symposium were collected in a brochure, published with an excellent set of graphics under the patronage of the Prime Minister, who delivered the opening words, of which no one remembered much, except that these fantastic events, beginning in a small country with great ambitions, took place right in midtown New York.

After the symposium, the Minister of Foreign Affairs came back to his office a defeated man. Even though it was already late, he found Gloria waiting for him. The well trained and devoted secretary instantly discerned his state of mind and made him herb tea in a Chinese porcelain cup painted with a dragon that somehow resembled the boa, except he was painted red The minister furrowed his eyebrows in distaste.

"And the snakeskin, what will become of it?" asked Gloria, pacing around it carefully but without hiding her admiration.

"Whatever you want," the minister capitulated and fell without much relish to reading the last URGENT letter. "Nothing to do but move on."

Two weeks later Gloria placed a pair of shiny pumps and a marvelous purse on the Minister's desk, both made of snake skin.

"For your wife," she whispered conspiratorially.

THE FUR HAT

Bob is a good, caring husband, though a bit boring. Case in point: before Betty went to Manhattan this morning, he made sure he told her several times, "Don't forget to put a scarf around your neck. It's bitter cold outside."

"My pullover will cover my neck nicely, thank you," she retorted.

"Still, you should take the scarf as well. That collar is not nearly enough to keep you warm."

"All right, all right, I'll take it," Betty sighed.

"What about the overcoat? Aren't you going to put it on? "

"No, I'll take the fur jacket instead."

"Your knees will freeze. Besides, that fur jacket is no good. Not without a hood, anyway. Better take your overcoat."

"What do I need a hood for? I'll just put on my fur hat. "

"Well, you can put your fur hat on, but you should also have a hood. You never know."

"That Russian fur hat is all I need, Bob. I bet it would keep me warm, even out there on the front line. "

"Well, take the overcoat, too. Do me a favor. I don't want to worry myself sick."

Betty gave in as usual. She was heading to Lenox Hill Hospital where a cousin of hers — well past sixty — was recovering from a hip replacement. She was going to bring her some pies and poppy seed coffee cake she had picked up at a Russian store in Queens, the borough where she and Bob had been living for more than twenty years.

"And watch your step. It's slippery out there," he added, as she positioned the fur hat on her head, wrapped the scarf around her neck, and pulled the hood on — all under his protective gaze.

"Jewish men make the best husbands," her mother had told her on several occasions. "They are good decent family men, down-to-earth and full of common sense. They know just how to take care of children and will not leave you, even though they might cheat on you from time to time."

There had been no children. Bob had taken good care of her, almost spoiling her in spite of his occasionally annoying possessiveness. He was a thoughtful, careful man, full of foresight, always trying to avoid danger in whatever form, lest he should tempt fate. He was fearful and prudent, avoiding the unknown, a man who felt at ease only in places and among people he knew very well. He was steady and prosaic, not given to adventure or great excitement, preferring the security of the commonplace and the blandness that left him feeling he was in control.

"You're boring me, Bob," Betty would often say to him. "Boy, you're such a nag!" And her voice, otherwise soft and pleasant, took on a Bovary-like desperation. "You know what? I'm capable of taking care of myself. Anyway, we can't go on living like this."

"Like what?"

"You know what I mean, this programmed kind of life, down to the smallest detail, always trying to avoid the slightest mishap; dodging everybody and everything."

These rebellious outbursts always put Bob in a funk. Thoroughly frightened, he would ask her plaintively, "Aren't we living the good life, Betty dear? Aren't you happy?"

Such tenderness was too much for Betty. She couldn't remain indifferent.

"But of course we do, dear. Ours is a very good life, and you are very kind man." Then she would say to herself. "I haven't had a chance to know anyone else. It's depressing to get old and realize you've been sleeping with the same man all your life. We shared a desk in high school, we let our romance blossom in college, and we ended up getting married before we graduated. What a beautiful woman I used to be! And now look at these bony, wizened hands. What a dreadful trick life plays on us!" she would continue to herself.

These thoughts crossed Betty's mind while riding the F train to Manhattan. The air was stuffy in the car, so she unwrapped her scarf and let her hood down. She decided she might as well keep the fur hat on. Why let people see the discolored, thinning, anemic remnants of her once blond hair? No doubt she had once been a flirt. She sighed and put her cheek next to the cold glass of the window and studied the faces around her.

Riding the Queens train is an experience. In each car there are at least ten nationalities. Today most of the passengers were wearing drab, gray clothes. They had long, tired faces. Some napped, their heads bobbing up and down, trying to hold a book or a newspaper printed in an outlandish language. Overhead were all sorts of advertisements — most of them in Spanish — offering legal assistance for accidents or medical injuries. In the end, Betty fell prey to the same drowsiness as the other passengers. She dozed off. It was just a few minutes, yet they felt like an eternity.

When she opened her eyes, she was perspiring slightly. Her face was flushed, and a thin rivulet of saliva ran down her chin. True, she had only slept a few minutes, but sensuously. The air in the car was hot. Across from her sat a tall, heavy-set man. He had a vacant scowl. No doubt, he had entered the train while she was asleep. And then she froze. She reached for her head and felt a lump in her throat. The hat was gone! She looked around, looked for it on the floor, but in vain. The hat was gone. And then she saw it. The man across from her was wearing it. He must have snatched it while she was asleep.

Fresh perspiration soaked her, caused by fear. She stared at him, a hulking man. Should she ask for her hat? Could she take a chance and cause a scandal in the train? What if the man responded violently? Naturally, he had not stolen it from her only to hand it back.

The train was pulling into the station. The man was dozing like other passengers, the hat sitting on top of his head. Betty screwed up her eyes, tensed her body, the way she used to in her youth when she competed in the broad jump. Then she chose her time carefully. At the last moment, just before the doors closed, she pounced like a cat, snatched it from the man's head, and dashed out just as the doors of the car closed behind her, leaving him numb with surprise.

She ran as fast as she could, abandoning her hospital visit to her cousin. She crossed the platform and boarded the train going in the opposite direction, heading home. Seeing her return so soon, Bob suspected something was wrong and, as was his want, panicked. Betty dropped into an armchair, drained of energy, clutching the recovered hat.

"You won't believe what just happened to me. I bet it would have frightened you to death if it had happened to you. Like in the movies."

"When I say you are naïve or that life is dangerous, you just laugh at me," Bob replied.

"A sinister-looking man — you ought to have seen him! — a

mountain with a shy look sat down — in from of me. I fell asleep and..." said Betty, letting the suspense build.

Bob was trembling, at the thought of what was to follow.

"Wait — just a minute," he implored. "Take off your coat. And your boots. Breathe deeply. Shall I get you a glass of water?"

As Betty took off her coat, out of the hood came the Russian fur hat, falling onto the floor. Bob picked it up and showed it to her triumphantly. "There! If it hadn't been for this hood, you'd have certainly lost the hat."

"What're you talking about?" snapped Betty. "Where did you get that hat?" she asked, continuing to clutch an identical Russian hat, though perhaps a little bigger.

"It must have dropped into the hood, while you were asleep," said Bob, smiling at the thought of what he had managed to prevent by insisting she take the hooded overcoat. Betty looked at him in horror.

For several weeks, the local Queens paper carried a notice about the Russian fur hat that had been found in the F train. No one called to claim it.

CONCESSION

Like most sculptors, he could have tried his hand at so-called decorative art — busts, statues, fake columns, flower baskets, little angels — or, reaping an even greater profit, garden sculpture: giant cast-iron frogs, fountains, stone deer, scary lions, or dramatic birds, little boys peeing or reading a bronze book on a cast iron bench — to please the taste of the rich Americans who pay big bucks to decorate their homes and backyards. Sasha, however, continued to sculpt what he pleased for himself and for the joy of his friends.

Viewing the work was a ritual, just as in Russia. It was, in fact, a Russia transported to New York, since one had the impression that everyone had escaped back here with their customs and everything intact. You could hear their accents all over the place.

His friends, most of them immigrant artists themselves, showed up at his studio, ate eggplant salad, marinated mushrooms, herring with onions and boiled potatoes, and drank vodka. They talked late into the night, nostalgically recalling how horrible life had been under communism and at the same time how great it had been, a paradox only Eastern European immigrants could understand, and this only when they were honest with themselves.

Here, as it had been in Russia, their art was in a kind of underground. If over there you had to resist political censorship in order to stay far from the mutilation of art during the socialist realist period, here you had to battle the ignorance that results from freedom of expression, culminating in kitsch and commercially driven taste. The monumentality of Stalinism, so despised in the East, found many disciples here. Being easily confused with grandeur, it satisfied the needs of this world of gigantic dimensions, its majesty and triumph.

Sasha was content with what he was doing. He went through powerful blue period, with melancholy moments of sadness and sentimentality when recalling the vast Russian taiga. He had a reddish beard and blue eyes, big hands and an even bigger appetite for life. He managed to survive somehow in his small studio in Brooklyn without sorrow for the past or plans for the future.

His wife complained a lot about his failure to promote his work, his lack of interest in making himself understood, and his inability to lure American buyers. "You have to accept, to make some concessions, learn to compromise, for God's sake, what's so wrong with that? We need to live, all things considered!" Eventually, she left him for a successful businessman who liked big bronze frogs — he ordered three to decorate his large garden.

One doesn't have to be an immigrant, an artist without a public, or a divorced man to experience on a rainy Sunday afternoon moments of uncertainty and dread, to feel crushing loneliness, to lie in bed, the phone on your chest, waiting for it to ring; to open your address book, leafing aimlessly from letter to letter in search of someone you might call at that impossible hour, someone who would also be interesting and intelligent, who could tell the difference between a bad case of the flu and a mere common cold.

So he called Victor, an essayist with a talent for writing who couldn't get a publisher yet. Usually on Sunday afternoons he read or translated from the Russian Romantics, and only after dusk was he drunk enough to compose his surrealistic poetry.

This time he was watching a Fellini movie. Sasha began to complain about this and that, saving his pet peeve for the end; it was really bugging him: his mid-life crisis, his inability to sell. Victor heard him out patiently, then offered him just enough sympathy to dry up some of the dramatic complaints pouring out of him, then gently led him to neutral territory, and fell into clichés.

"Do you know how many people are on Prozac in this country? Do you see how many talk to themselves on the street? The alienation in big cities is not just the title of a soap opera. Well, you're in the most powerful city of all. You need time to get in step with its madness, its magic. But you're in the right place."

Sasha grumbled. He had heard this speech about New York over and over. Victor sensed his disappointment and changed his tone.

"After all, it's just a rainy Sunday. They're the same everywhere."

He was clearly eager to return to Fellini.

"We, the exiled ones, are built like nomads, we dream in atrophied languages, and, naturally, sometimes we're overwhelmed by a sort of uselessness, a kind of fatigue. The search is never over, especially when you think that you've found what you're looking for. Stop thinking. Even this exile can be simplified somehow. Some are meant to leave, just as others are meant to stay. And the one who leaves is not necessarily the one who's having a hard time in his native land, and the one who stays is not necessarily the privileged one. We're wanderers. But something might come out of our drifting after all."

Sasha wasn't following him anymore. He was sick of theories. Out the window he watched Bedford Avenue completely deserted that Sunday afternoon. The rain had cleaned everything, the pavement sparkled, and the people had disappeared. Only a few cabs drove by, and occasionally the siren of an ambulance made soothing sounds for him, obscuring Victor's voice. A Korean arranged flowers in vases in the small corner deli. A gray, violet light reflected off the glass of the Thai restaurant across the street. An old homeless person pushed a supermarket cart filled with empty plastic bottles. A sort of languor overcame him.

He heard Victor telling him imperatively:

"Go out, wrap up some works, and show them to a gallery. I'm serious. Did you ever try? There are dozens in uptown Manhattan. Start with these. You'll see, you'll feel better. What have you to loose? They might be interested, you never know."

After living in New York for a while, Victor had moved a few years ago to a college in California, where he taught art history. From time to time he would come back east to give a lecture or to attend a translation seminar, and then he and Sasha would talk for hours, chain-smoking and reminiscing about the old country where no one gave a hoot about the ozone layer, cholesterol, jogging, fitness, body-building, or anything of the sort. No pressing concern there to have one's annual check-up. Back then life was a long, satisfying conversation over glasses of vodka or any cheap — but strong — alcohol, and overflowing ashtrays.

"Listen to me, why don't you go right now? Go and show them some real work, man!"

Like a robot, Sasha shoved his portfolio under his arm, wrapped three sculptures in blankets, and went to the subway. He went uptown to the galleries that Victor insisted he knew were interested in contemporary art.

The first place he saw made a good impression. Both rooms had works by Chagall, Matisse, and Picasso, while in the center were some small sculptures by Diego Giacometti and Henry Moore. Perfect, thought Sasha, and after strolling leisurely through the rooms, he took advantage of the fact that he was the only visitor and approached the elderly lady behind the beautiful rosewood desk who seemed to be in charge.

"Sir?" the lady said to him before Sasha had time to open his mouth.

"It's a very beautiful gallery," began Sasha awkwardly.

"It's British!" she apostrophized, as though British were a synonym for "very beautiful."

"Of course, British, I realize that," Sasha stuttered, smiling in order to break the ice.

"Sir, I have work to do," she replied, barely moving her thin lips. "If there's nothing else I can do to help you, then please excuse me."

"I'm an artist as well," Sasha jumped in.

The lady's face grew icy.

"Sculptor."

"So?"

She looked bored as she picked up a cup of antique English porcelain and sipped her tea. Sasha unwrapped two of the statues and placed them on the British desk.

"As a matter of fact, I'd like to show you some work."

"Why?"

"You might be interested."

"I'm only interested in the dead. Certainly you must have noticed that we only exhibit the dead here."

"Don't you think you're limiting your public?"

"Public?"

"The buyers, I mean."

"We're not interested in what you call *buyers*. We have our *clients*. *They* prefer the dead. They are the only secure investment."

"And you don't want to discover new artists, still in the prime of their power, or at the height of their artistic potential? Perhaps they too would one day be a profitable investment, don't you think?"

"That day you're referring to comes only after they've passed into the next world."

"Ma'am, it's not like that. There are plenty of famous artists who are still alive, very highly valued, and whose pieces are bought by agents and collected by galleries."

"Perhaps, but I'm not aware of any. Our gallery isn't interested in them."

"Please forgive my insisting, but you can't base your entire collection on the dead."

"That's exactly what I've been doing for forty years, sir."

"Well, then since I'm alive, what do you expect me to do?"

"That's your problem, sir. I'm sorry I can't help you."

Sasha returned her strange look, wrapped up his pieces, which the lady hadn't even bothered to look at politely, thanked her, and left. The cool spring wind filled his massive chest, billowed his long hair and reddish beard. He lit a cigarette and felt powerful and healthy. He loved New York in the spring, despite the withered ladies hidden in British galleries of the Upper West Side, who took an interest in you only if you were dead. And he had no desire to commit suicide. Not today.

He went into another gallery, which was surely American. The young lady inside smiled incessantly and had a square plastic water bottle next to the catalogues on her desk. She wore comfortable, practical shoes that allowed her to spend the day on her feet, sauntering from one room to the next, handing out information, engaging visitors in conversations, acting distractedly amiable. When you spoke to her she looked at you but wasn't there. She smiled at you but didn't understand exactly what you were asking. She stared through you into the void with an exaggeratedly amiable manner.

"Hi! Can I help you?"

Sasha unwrapped his pieces and set them on the desk one by one. The woman smiled encouragingly.

"I am an artist. Sculptor. I was thinking you might be interested in my work."

"O great, great! Where are you from?"

"Russia."

"Wonderful. Fabulous."

"Would you like to take a look at my portfolio? These are some of the pieces I've made in the last three years."

"Certainly. Oh, they're fabulous. Great."

"I have others like them in bronze."

"Hmm, hmm. Cool."

"What do you think?"

"They're really...interesting," she said, even before she had time to look. "I like this wolf," she continued, running her hand over one of the pieces Sasha had set next to her square plastic water bottle. "It's a wolf, right?"

"Yes, a wolf," said Sasha, happily.

He also liked this piece very much. He turned it to face the woman, who continued to study it thoughtfully. Sasha was excited. Something was about to happen.

"Bronze?"

"Certainly, bronze."

"Well, you know, I might just have a buyer for it."

"Great. It would be great." Sasha's eyes sparkled.

"There's just one a little problem, I hope it won't bother you too much. Can I make a suggestion?"

"Certainly, certainly," Sasha encouraged her, feeling like he would promise her anything.

"Could you add a little girl?"

"A little girl?"

"You know, like in Little Red Riding Hood. I wanted to say it, but I thought it might shock you. Could you sculpt a Little Red Riding Hood next to the wolf?"

"Ma'am, miss, I don't understand."

"I know it seems weird to ask. And I don't mean in any way to offend you as an artist. But if it's not too much trouble to ask, I've got a great buyer for you. For over twenty years he's been collecting Little Red Riding Hoods. He's a reliable client. I've already sold him fourteen pieces. He's got an impressive collection. He'd buy your piece right away, at a price, believe me, that you'd never get anywhere else. All you have to do is to add a Little Red Riding Hood. Wolves alone don't interest him.

Sasha's ears were turning red. He stared at the wolf, which he'd worked on for several months, and tender affection filled his body. He wasn't angry or insulted; he simply loved his piece more than ever.

"Well, what do you think?"

"Miss, I don't know what to tell you. I don't do Little Red Riding Hoods."

"I know, I know, but try to understand what I'm asking. A little, how can I put it, concession, I wouldn't call it a compromise, just a little concession. How can it hurt you, just to add a Little Red Riding Hood next to this wolf? It wouldn't cost you anything, and the return would be phenomenal. Besides, you may come up with a Little Red Riding Hood that you'd love yourself. Don't you think there could be Little Red Riding Hoods that are masterpieces? Think about it."

"I've thought about it for a long time. For twenty years I've been thinking about it. Certainly, what you're asking is no big thing. A little while ago someone suggested that I need to be dead before my work could be taken into consideration. You only want a Little Red Riding Hood. Maybe I can do it"

"Fabulous. Great."

"I would do it if I had a few lives ahead of me. I would spend one of them sculpting only Little Red Riding Hoods."

The woman withdrew a few steps, smiling nervously. "I hope you didn't take this the wrong way. I honestly wanted to help you."

"Are you interested in any other of my pieces?"

"I'm afraid not. Though they're fabulous. Absolutely fabulous," she said nervously.

"I thank you very much."

"Much luck. Have a great day."

As he was about to walk out of the gallery, Sasha's eyes fell on the inscription hanging above the door: "True artists speak about themselves as if they were dead."

"Can you tell me who said this?" he asked the lady while a shiver ran down his spine.

"I don't remember his name. British, I think," she answered, the billboard smile still on her face, growing.

"British, certainly."

Sasha crossed the street, more alive than ever. He held his heavy pieces to his chest, protectively, possessively. Through his clothes he felt the cold metal that had taken the shape his hands gave it.

PARKING

Finally, I was to meet Lisa. We had postponed our introduction several times. Something always came up in her schedule and at the last moment we'd have to cancel and reschedule. This evening, though, she called to confirm. 8pm sharp at her place. "Don't be late," she cautioned. Was it because she knew I came from a country where people were not famous for punctuality? Or maybe she had no idea where I came from. Maybe my accent wasn't so thick on the phone. I didn't know what Dominique had told her about me.

In any event, I don't like to be late. I decided to drive to her place on the Upper West Side in my new used car that I'd just bought from a dealer in Queens. I filled my pockets with quarters so that I could park on the street and tossed into my bag a magazine with some of my poems that I'd managed to get published. I wanted to write a dedication to Lisa, but I didn't know her full name. All Dominique had told me was, "You have to see Lisa." And I hadn't asked for more. He is familiar with this world, and I trust him fully.

I was looking forward to this meeting with more than a little anticipation. Lisa had assumed all sorts of dimensions in my mind. I put a great deal of hope in her and lots of illusions played tricks on my mind. I even thought I could achieve my dream of becoming a published author in this new, foreign, vast culture. Wasn't I coming to a country where dreams are fulfilled? Here miracles can occur any moment, and success can come overnight, I had been told. After all, Eastern Europe where I came from was ridding itself of communism, and that was miraculous too.

I heard Dominique telling me imperatively, "You've got to see

Lisa."

"Lisa?"

"Yeah, a friend of mine. Very talented, intelligent, with lots of connections. You'll like her. And I think she will like you, too."

I couldn't think of anything in particular that Dominique had told me about Lisa, but in my mind I somehow associated her with the literary world. I was left with the impression that she might possibly offer me some advice, some precious bits of information on how I could make it to the seemingly inaccessible world of publishing. Or, who knows, she might be a writer herself. And so there I was, dutifully bringing the magazine featuring my first poems translated into English and published — the only breakthrough I could claim since immigrating to America.

I arrived in front of Lisa's apartment building on the Upper West Side by seven thirty and searched in vain for an empty parking space. Worried, I looked at my watch. It was well past eight, and Lisa's warnings against being late rang in my ears, now with bitter irony. Embarrassed, I called her.

"I'm terribly sorry. I've been looking for a parking space for half an hour now."

"We'll be waiting for you. And don't worry, you'll find parking soon." Lisa assured me calmly.

Her words sounded a bit strange. "And why *we*?" So she wasn't alone. Maybe a friend or a husband? I'd barely hung up, when the jeep in front of me pulled out. I quickly parked with a sigh of relief, blessing gold-mouthed Lisa. I crossed the wide avenue to the building's entrance and in less than two minutes was ringing the doorbell to her apartment, panting with sheer exhaustion, nervousness, and conflicting emotions.

Lisa opened the door and looked at me as if she had known me a long time. I did the same. She was small, moving forward with graceful movements, displaying the most mysterious smile I'd ever seen. Her face took on various expressions as her smile gradually spread across her face. It didn't start at the corners of her mouth but rather in the middle of her slightly pursed lips. Her eyebrows arched, and two lines creased her forehead. She kept switching from a child-like air of innocence to the stiff image of a tough teacher. As her smile broadened, her cheeks took on a rosy hue, and her face relaxed.

I felt as if she could change from a shy teenager exuding candor and naiveté into a wizened, skeptical intellectual in a moment, hovering between curiosity and irony. In the end a little woman was scrutinizing me inquisitively. Lisa's unforgettable smile melted into an air of warm authority with which she studied me over the black rims of her glasses. She took my hand.

"We've all been waiting for you," she said, leading the way into the living room.

About a dozen women looked up at me. They were sitting on sofas and couches in front of coffee tables. Suddenly I was gripped by fear. So many women gathered in one place, all waiting for me? I barely felt able to take another step, but Lisa gently pushed me forward. The ladies were sizing me up, as if to assess whether I met their expectations.

I sat on the nearest sofa, eager to avoid more scrutiny, having already sinned by arriving late. It was then that I realized that the blonde woman next to me was barefoot. I looked around. They were all barefoot. All their shoes were aligned in a neat row along the wall. Do I really have to? I gave Lisa a quick, apprehensive glance, and she, as if reading my mind, nodded a benevolent "yes; no problem, you can keep your shoes on."

Lisa was seated on a tall chair, a kind of stool, dominating the group. She, too, kept her shoes on. Full of mystery, she broke into another broad smile, which I didn't know how to interpret. Then she asked everyone to introduce herself for my sake, since they seemed to know one another well. A photographer here, a social studies teacher there, an editor, a retired go-go dancer now comfortably transformed into a distinguished-looking housewife, a real-estate agent, a singer, a fashion designer, and so on. Dominique had been right: Lisa did have lots of connections.

The room was permeated with the atmosphere of a classroom or a conference hall, which at that moment was the last thing I needed. Hadn't I come all primed up for an intimate tête-à-tête with Lisa? Could this be a meeting of a feminist consciousness-raising group? I felt as if I could strangle Dominique.

Each woman stated her name, age, profession, family background, and her idea of a good time, peppering her presentations with bitter, caustic remarks about her past divorces or current solitude. Others betrayed their deep-seated fear of aging or the usual dread of loneliness. Lisa came over and laid her hand on my shoulder. Her gestures were natural and tender.

"Do you chant?"

Caught unprepared, after a moment wondering why I had been asked such a strange question, I responded with a smile, "Of course I chat. Everybody does, right?"

Lisa gave me a gratified smile. "You think so?"

"Isn't that what we're doing right now?"

I had no idea what I was talking about, but my words were making a good impression.

"And who taught you to do it?"

"Oh, it runs in the family," I answered confidently. "I've been doing it ever since I was a little girl, with great results. I've always had a sociable nature, boosted, no doubt, by my Latin temperament." I was trying to sound good-natured and jolly, but I could not understand why they were elevating the simple art of conversation.

"I didn't know that the Latin temperament was an advantage," said the lady next to me as she rubbed her bare feet against each other.

Then Lisa put an end to all the whispering, buzzing, and rustling that usually goes on whenever a bunch of women get together, and announced in a tone of great authority, "Well, shall we start, then?"

It sounded like an order. I felt uncomfortable, thinking that I had to talk, probably a lot, in my poor English with my bad accent.

Lisa lit two sticks of incense and opened some sort of wooden box attached to the wall. A deep hush fell over the audience; all eyes fixed intently on it. I rose, meaning to take a closer look at it, but the blonde next to me stopped me with a gesture that brooked no opposition. She whispered into my ear, "It's a *gohonzon*"

"A... what?" I inquired with a feeling that my English was getting worse.

"Actually, I don't know exactly," she confessed. "They call it *gohonzon*. I believe it's a Sanskrit word."

"A sort of icon?" I tried.

"I guess! Something like that."

Each of the women pulled from her handbag a little book, turned to the first page and wrapped a string of colored beads around her fingers, then settled into a more comfortable position.

Lisa, the conductor, with an incense stick in her hand, clinked a little bell, and all of them started chanting in unison. "NA-MIO-HO-RENGE-KYO." These syllables were chanted again and again in the same cadence and rhythm, while each lady rubbed her string of beads between her fingers.

I realized they weren't chatting. I'd blurted out that I was an expert only to discover now that, actually, I had no idea what to do. I'd dropped in on this session wholly by accident and was now forced to play along, lest they discover the truth about me. So I kept mumbling on, as best I could, trying, but not entirely succeeding, to stay in tune with the others, sometimes failing miserably, skipping many beats, all the time hoping I could hide from them the truth — namely, that I hadn't the slightest idea what was going on here — I, who had never chanted anything in my life.

I realized how unprepared I was for the life of this city. How could I dream of getting published here? I couldn't even understand the basics. My dream was slowly vanishing along with the syllables that I could barely pronounce.

The blonde woman next to me held out the little book halfway between us, pointing to each line with her finger as it was being chanted, encouraging me to fall into step with the other chanters. Then she placed her string of beads on my fingers, hoping this might somehow improve my performance. But it was no use. I was a disaster. The women kept uttering those dreary syllables in increasingly loud, shrill voices in a chorus that sounded both dramatic and languorous. They kept this up for almost twenty minutes.

That little book contained nothing but those same syllables, over and over, with pauses and changes of rhythm. How I would have liked to see additional words of that strange language, but the chorus wailed on its lugubrious chant, some of the women uttering the syllables in a high-pitched voice, while others apparently fell into a deep trance.

Here and there a voice had become irritatingly loud; one or two had apparently lost all of their saliva, and nearly all had eyes that threatened to pop out of their sockets, as, with a fixed stare, they diligently followed the enigmatic string of words.

I felt provincial and lost in this sophisticated gathering. I was definitely ignorant, unable to see anything magical in their chant, and felt ridiculous for not noticing meditation or spiritual uplift.

I remembered a similar moment that I experienced as a child in my tiny country in Eastern Europe when my grandmother took me from my playground on a beautiful Sunday morning and brought me with her to the church where she forced me to kneel, to be silent, and to listen to an endless mass. While she was praying with her eyes closed, a mysterious smile illuminated her face. A smile very similar to Lisa's.

Although this female choir had at first made me curious, eventually it became just boring. My only hope was that their Sanskrit chanting would somehow rouse the ire of the neighbors, who would come to the door and stop all this racket.

More than half an hour later, Lisa clinked the bell again and the chorus came to an abrupt stop. They all looked exhausted but happy. Lisa beamed her benign approbation, pleased with their overall performance, and, from the haughty elevation of her chair, asked me, "How was it?"

"Very good."

"How are you feeling?"

"Oh, great, just great."

"You may come every week, if you want."

"Sure… we'll talk about it on the phone," I mumbled and attempted to rise.

"We'll stay a little longer," Lisa explained. "These are the choicest moments."

The women seemed quite relaxed, content, and, above all, relieved. Some of them kept their eyes half closed as if they'd just wakened from a pleasant dream. Others were staring open-eyed, as if they were seeing the world for the first time. Obviously the chanting had had a different impact on each of them. Only Lisa maintained the same controlled expression, the same mysterious smile.

"It's in our power to save ourselves," she told one of them, handing her a thick book.

They started to talk chaotically. The word "harmony" popped up several times. A cell phone rang, and its owner turned it off in disgust. "He doesn't understand that my life has changed."

It wasn't clear who. She may have been referring to the man who'd just telephoned. Several others nodded, smiling sympathetically.

"I'm a free woman, I've recovered my power, and I'm in tune with the universal harmony."

Lisa watched her contentedly. I fumbled around, betraying my impatience, and handed the string of beads back to my neighbor.

"You may keep them, if you wish," she said, generously. "I have several more at home. There are a hundred and eight in all. Do you know what they stand for?" she tested me, taking pride in having this bit of information to share. "They are earth-bound wishes chanted away into the realm of cosmic energy."

"Do these wishes ever come true?" I asked politely.

"Of course they do. Look, when you called earlier, unable to find a parking place, Lisa asked us to chant for you. And sure enough, shortly afterwards your wish came true, didn't it? Miraculously, you found a spot right away, did you not?"

"It's true," I said, bewildered.

She looked at me triumphantly.

"You'll see how many problems you can solve by chanting," she added.

I said my good-byes to the barefoot ladies, thanking my neighbor for her kindness, and gave Lisa a hug. She walked me to the door, unable to conceal her displeasure at my leaving so soon. I couldn't bring myself to look her straight in the eye. Just as I was about to walk out, she planted a kiss on the corner of my mouth and smiled mysteriously. I forgot all about giving her the magazine with my poems.

When I reached my car I found a parking ticket for $55 under my wiper. My time had expired. It hadn't crossed my mind to chant for that.

LITTLE PEOPLE

America had settled for blooming prosperity. For a good while now, the stock market had been riding high, unemployment had dipped spectacularly, and gasoline prices had been within reason. People were building and traveling.

Andrei Roscov, a New Yorker naturalized more than fifteen years before, had won his battles with immigration. He had fought his way up the professional ladder and had reached as far as his training and capabilities allowed. All he was left with now was the savor of his success. He was past his prime with only retirement to look forward to.

As the great confrontations were behind him, he started to think of ways to spend his old age. He was mildly terrified at the thought of inaction, which could undo men both physically and psychologically. In a way, he had already started to prepare for retirement, trying out hobbies, dabbling in things that he would later practice as antidotes to solitude, to the punishment of having to stay at home all day even if this home were his dreamy upstate possession complete with his relatively well tempered and rather understanding wife.

He could travel, but then, how much can one really travel? After all, how many movies can one see, how many chess games can one play, how much can one garden? Besides, he didn't play golf or tennis; he wasn't the athletic type. Then again, there's always the book. One can read books forever. Reading is a sure thing, readily available and potentially endless. All he had to do was to recover all the books he had put off reading, all the books he had failed to read all those years he had to wage war with life, all those years he had to work until late in the evenings and then collapsed in exhaustion.

Andrei Roscov read not just randomly but systematically. Books by classic and contemporary authors, expensive volumes, and cheap editions soon began to flood the house, which until recently harbored few books, mostly those bought by the children during their college years. Andrei Roscov became a conscientious book buyer, a regular at local libraries.

He would read insatiably, devouring universal literature chronologically from the Greeks to post-modern authors, going through all the major literary schools and periods. He discovered fascinating writers and entered a world he never imagined to be so replete.

Books flooded his home. All the rooms sprung shelves, wall units, and all manner of custom-made or improvised places for book storage. Books were practically everywhere: on top of tables, spread on couches, in the kitchen, under the bed.

His wife seemed puzzled in the beginning, but by now she had accepted the odd development as a harmless childish obsession or fancy: her husband had suddenly chosen to become an overeducated eccentric.

Andrei Roscov would use every free moment for reading. He would read on the subway, at the dinner table, on the toilet, in the garden, even at the stadium, when he'd go to baseball games. He had been a passionate baseball fan in the old days, but now he was dismayed by games that lasted a long time and kept him away from his reading.

He would read during the weekends, late into the night, and early in the mornings before leaving for work. He would read at work, too, during his lunch hour, while munching on a sandwich, or whenever he found a moment of peace and quiet. Since he had been promoted to department head in the fiber optics company where he worked, he no longer did his job in a cubicle but had his own office away from his colleagues' prying eyes, from the constant shuffling of papers, and the irrepressible chatter of computer keyboards. He was free now to read as soon as he was alone in his office with major emergencies out of the way. He naturally hid his books in drawers and avoided being caught reading by colleagues or bosses.

He read avidly, thinking how unfair it is to have only one life with all the millions of books ever written. He felt frustrated by the volumes that would be left unopened, by the books that would survive him unread, by the authors he would not be able to reach. He adored the feel of hard covers, the feel of freshly cut paper and of pages weathered by the passage of time; he loved to leaf through vanilla-scented volumes and to behold the very shape and feel of rare books.

Many antiquarians began to know him. They would set aside editions for him that they thought he might be interested in, though in fact Andrei Roscov was interested in simply everything, in every work of literature. He had naturally acquired some taste and already preferred certain authors, genres, and themes, but his reading hunger obliged him to refrain from nothing from poetry to drama, philosophy to fiction. He was riveted by reading, by the succulence of words. His hands shivered on the spines of books and his eyes raced insatiably from one word to the next and from one line to the other.

His desperate advance on culture had started to take its toll — not just in terms of money but also in sleepless nights that left obsessive dark circles under his eyes, eye infections, and exhaustion.

He checked the stock market less and less frequently even though he had been a successful investor with good intuition and a knack for the brokerage business. There had been a time when he called himself a market fiend. He had made substantial profits on the stock market and had achieved financial stability precisely because of it. Now, however, all he did was to spend ever-increasing sums of money. He saw money in a new light — it seemed to have been made only to be invested in books.

Old age no longer scared him. Neither did retirement, whose monotony and promise of decrepitude are so terrifying to so many men. He was now looking forward to his retirement, to devoting all his time to reading.

Roscov did not exhibit any other bizarre traits. He did not become moody or unstable. He was just the mirror of his reading. Whenever he was reading philosophy or was deep into existentialism or minimalism, he would become sad, withdrawn, depressed and would refuse to talk or eat. For him, as for the dejected absurdist or pessimistic writers he was reading at the time, the world lost its meaning.

On the other hand, whenever he read romances, he would become melancholy, even maudlin, his eyes became tender, obscured by an avalanche of sentimental clichés. Then again, his condition became more serious when he turned to fantastic or surrealist authors. At such times, he simply wanted to fly away. But all this happened within the confines of normality. He continued to control his moods, which tended to be rather histrionic.

Roscov had become skilled at walking the tightrope between reality and the ineffable. He had become a mime capable of playing all possible roles, and there seemed to be too little time for the countless roles and existential moods from the boredom of a Madame Bovary to Chekhovian nostalgia, from Hamlet-like indecision to the hallucinations of "life as a dream."

Most of the time, though, he would appear pensive or grave, since he was constantly under the spell of the events or characters in whatever book he happened to be reading. The angles of his face had grown sharper, his eyes had acquired a glimmer of wisdom, and his fingers appeared longer like those of a piano player constantly practicing his skills, maybe because Roscov himself was increasingly turning page after page in the grand score of literature.

He was becoming mannered, stylish, aristocratic, meditative, and enigmatic. At times he would appear to plumb the meaning of existence in depth, to penetrate the complexity of life, indeed of the whole universe, to ask fundamental questions, and to be concerned with the purpose and destiny of all mankind — where we come from, what we are meant to do, how, why, and until when.

Death, mysterious and incommensurable, a fat subject for most of the authors Roscov was reading, had also carved out a space for itself among his preferred themes for reflection. For him, death was both revelation and forgiveness, end point and ultimate accomplishment, the doppelgänger of our lives, the shadow awaiting to engulf us.

When his thoughts bent towards death, he would be attracted by metaphysics and would represent death as a wise woman bored by earthly entropy, a cynical apparition in a smoky mirror or behind a closing door. Roscov was at times resigned, at times alarmed.

He would strain to feel death's touch on his shoulder during those long autumn nights when everything is still and settled, when leaves rustle and daylight gradually slips away into the calm and cool night filled with the sweet smells of fruit and smoke. He would sit on his porch facing the woods, and he would read while listening to the silence and fancying himself as Raskolnikoff, Mishkin, or Gregor Samsa. At such times, nothing in his future had the power to terrify him.

Literature gave him strength; it manipulated his personality and made him stronger precisely because of the flexibility he gained by inhabiting so many characters. He had room enough for them all. He could take any shape without losing interest in new readings, without being enslaved by any of his experiences, except by reading itself, by reading as a global phenomenon indispensable to life itself, by reading as a definitive, organic action. He grew increasingly certain that he would die if he did not read. All this, at a time when no one was dreaming of classic heroes anymore, when the contemporaneous characters with whom most people identified were superheroes turned millionaires overnight, actors, singers, brokers, corporate lawyers, and internet moguls. The world was turning into a gigantic dot-com. Multi-media slowly replaced books; cyber-space replaced the space of literature bit by bit.

Perhaps Andrei Roscov's destiny was to keep classical values alive, to remember those powerful characters that changed the history of culture, to rekindle the glory of the words written by the great titans of literature.

With whom could Andrei Roscov share all these thoughts? Who could understand him, who could believe him? But then again, he had no need for anyone's understanding; he did not seek approval or appreciation for his gigantic gesture of spiritual elevation. He felt at home with his books. All he wanted was to read, to be left alone to read.

He was conspiring with time as best he could. He made short order of his social, professional, and family obligations. The minimum, nothing more. What was left of his life was his own, and he would make use of it by reading. He had no screw loose; he was not alienated, though all that culture, stored higgledy-piggledy inside him, could have easily brought him estrangement or eeriness. He was a well balanced man who had turned one of his hobbies into a vice — a vice both healthy and beneficial, a fabulous vice!

One night Jesus came into Andrei Roscov's dreams. The apparition was doubtless due to his readings, which leaned at the time more towards philosophy and the history of religions. Anyway, Jesus was dressed in his famous white mantle with wide flowing sleeves; he was sad and benign with a halo hovering over his head, a classic image derived from paintings, frescoes, and naïve book illustrations. He looked rather like a chosen beggar bathed in resplendent light. He was holding a book and a strange pencil radiating light from its tip.

At each move, the tip of the pencil would spring words toward him, themselves made of light, although material, carnal, heavy, with distinctive shapes, floating like fantastic luminous birds. They would unfurl in the air, and for a fraction of a second, Roscov could read them, but then they would disappear. He beheld words written on air and was fascinated by their blinding pulsation, by how they vanished only to be replaced by yet others endlessly pouring from the tip of the pencil, held by Jesus like a sword.

He was at first scared by the apparition, especially since it was so faithful to the images he already knew. Jesus appeared real, true, a living man, and Roscov could not understand the meaning of that rare encounter, and he especially could not understand what Jesus wanted of him.

He had read that only the elect few have such dreams and that they are rarely without consequences. Those dreaming are usually given messages, tasks to perform, duties to fulfill, some kind of cross to bear. He was relieved to see that Jesus was not speaking to him, that he was not pushing him to understand anything beyond the spectacle of his apparition, that he was not burdening him with any kind of cross or commandments, that he did not ask anything of him.

He was beginning to believe that Jesus had not even noticed his presence when the Savior made a sudden move, pointing the shining tip of the pen towards Roscov. He stretched out his hands, thinking that Jesus was offering him the pencil, but Jesus rushed on, piercing Roscov's heart with it.

Roscov instantly woke up, feeling his chest inundated by words. It wasn't painful. He even had a strange and pleasant feeling of plenitude. He closed his eyes and almost saw Jesus walking towards a milky horizon, stepping lightly as if he were walking on water or flying low above the ground, as if he were walking on one of those gliding planes in an airport.

Roscov was left confused, his chest brimming with words, overwhelmed by the strangeness of the heritage the divine apparition had lodged in his heart, though he did not try to understand its meaning. Nor did he talk to anyone about it. He went back to his books. He was reading perhaps more eagerly than ever, now that Jesus had clearly shown him that words were born out of light, that light and words were one. He had finally understood why God said that in the beginning was the Word.

Roscov was now hiding under his shirt all the luminous words thrust by the Savior straight into his heart. He discovered that it wasn't all that difficult to live with such riches in one's heart. Roscov's life hadn't changed in the least. Soon he would forget to think about his dream, caught in his web of minor and major readings.

Were his mother alive, she would have been so happy to see him buried in books. All his childhood, she had tried unsuccessfully to encourage him to read.

He had been born in a small town in Eastern Europe, where Hungarians, Germans, Romanians, and Jews lived peacefully together except for those few tensions that usually sprang out of one too many drinks. His father, a history teacher, was an unsophisticated salt-of-the-earth fellow with robust ideas about duty, family, and correctness. He was as conscientious about his work at the school as he was about his life at home. He was a man one could count on, but there was little to talk with him about outside of the specifics of his everyday life. Andrei Roscov had invigorating yet vague memories of him. His father had left little in the way of an impression; he was just a reliable memory and nothing more.

His mother, on the other hand, had been a real character, a complicated figure in his life. He wondered how she came to be in that gray, unexceptional town lodged between the mountains. She played the piano and she had a real talent for drawing; during the winter in their small kitchen she would paint long male faces in surreal settings and short pudgy women with wings or unicorn horns. She spoke five languages and was a passionate reader. Andrei Roscov remembered her reading, always. She could do anything, a sophisticated lady who concerned herself with the arts and ideas circulating throughout Europe. She would come up with unexpected insights; she was subtle and humorous, a flying spirit in the sleepy provincial town where they lived.

Roscov was very proud of her. But he was sometimes intimidated by her tenacity, by her alert spirit, and had a hard time meeting her expectations. He was tortured and guilty about not being always able to rise to the challenge.

He felt that he was disappointing her in being so normal, so ordinary, so bent on refusing to read, so wayward and uninterested in anything but his games and his friends, so lacking in any special passion, so exasperated by his mother's ambitions to see him become one of the elect few. He did not have it in him to collect prizes, and it didn't look as if he had a chance of becoming any kind of champion soon.

It was because of his mother that their house was filled to the brim with books in all sorts of languages and about all sorts of things. Andrei Roscov, though, treated the books as furniture, not to be moved lest one tried to threaten the good order and tidiness of the house. The more his mother encouraged him to read and the more books she piled on him, the stronger Andrei's rejection and resistance.

When he was fifteen, his mother died. She passed away uneasy about leaving a disoriented and unformed child in this world despite all her efforts to transfer to him at least part of her heritage. So far it hadn't worked. Andrei Roscov took after his father, who for a while seemed to him an easier model to follow. He had admired his mother without really understanding her, but he had never wanted to follow the ambitious dreams she had carved out for him.

This was all about to come to a head after the fall of the Berlin

Wall. Up to that point, he had lived inside the communist system without ever trying to rebel, without ever doing anything courageous. He had resigned himself to the pervasive collective cowardice of his time and place. He had graduated from one of the technical institutes of higher education, had been married, and had brought forth two children. He was a member of the majority class of which little was expected other than quiet survival in the given historical circumstances.

But Roscov, instead of completing his monotonous existence in the now liberated Eastern Europe, decided to challenge his destiny. He immigrated to the United States with his wife and two children, and started all over again. This proved to be a courageous, daring gesture, especially since he was no longer in the prime of youth and had little to go on other than his unspectacular tenacity. But he succeeded.

He was the first in his family to set foot in America; still, he worked his way into a middle-class existence and became a respectable citizen of the most important world power. He could imagine his mother smiling contently wherever she was — not so much because of his success in America, as because of the reading — to which he had recently dedicated his life. That was the one thing he was sure of.

In the evenings, he went to readings and book signings, to meetings with authors who promoted their books in stores and book clubs. He had purchased a long white scarf that he twisted with studied negligence over his elegant coat, modeling himself after a recently discovered character with a complex psychological makeup.

It was on one of these evenings that he met the great Allen

Hunter, an established writer and author of several novels, some of which had been awarded prestigious prizes. He was waiting in line at a Barnes & Noble in Manhattan for Hunter to autograph a copy of his latest work.

When Roscov finally reached the front of the line and spelled out his name so the author could add it to a canned formula such as "with regards," Hunter lifted his eyes inquiringly. "Andrei Roscov? The name sounds familiar."

"No, I don't think..." Roscov grew self-conscious. "I'm not a literary... type. That is, well, I mean, I don't think you could have met me before."

"Not sure... Roscov with a C or a K?"

"C."

"You never wrote or published?"

"Never," Roscov assured him, a bit embarrassed by the long line of people waiting for autographs behind him. Allen Hunter couldn't have cared less.

"Still, Andrei Roscov....I definitely heard or read the name before. No writers in the family?"

"Well, my mother used to correspond with all sorts of literary types. But... I don't think, she wasn't really a writer."

"Where are you from?"

"That's not going to help either. I'm from Eastern Europe."

"Oh, my grandmother was from Bukovina! Listen, if you can wait a few minutes, I'll finish up here and we can go have a drink. I know a place nearby. If you don't mind, that is."

Roscov was speechless. An invitation from the great Allen Hunter himself! He suddenly remembered the words of an old fortune teller in his hometown many years before. He had never given them a second thought, since he had no inclination for superstition.

The family had been to a cousin's wedding. Towards the morning hours, when everyone's mind had turned cloudy with alcohol, food, and music, an old fortune teller was brought in to go from table to table. His wife kept goading him to show his palm to the fortune teller, and Roscov played along halfheartedly. People moved languidly, disoriented, like women whose mascara has begun to run at the end of a prolonged party, like men mumbling with their ties loosened and their white shirt sleeves rolled up among cigarette smoke and alcohol.

The fortune teller told him that at the mid-point of his life his destiny was to break off suddenly and take an unexpected path. It looked, she said, almost as if this were another life, a new one, which Roscov was to experience with intensity as if he had died and been reborn as a new man, with a new calling, in a new world.

He did get a bit scared but later decided that there was no reason to give any credence to the old fortune teller, who probably said whatever crossed her mind to the wedding guests waiting in line for her prophecies. But she did tell him that his life would be influenced by his meeting a famous man, a celebrity, and that things would change under his spell.

He had first remembered the words of the fortune teller when he arrived in America; he thought that that was the change she had foreseen. Now he was making a new set of connections. Maybe the life the old lady had told him about was his life as a reader, and the famous man was Allen Hunter himself. Or could it be Jesus from his dreams?

But beyond these speculations, superstitions, and coincidences, Roscov and Hunter were about to embark on a friendship with unexpected consequences for the passionate reader Roscov had become.

The bar Hunter had mentioned was two blocks from the bookstore where they had met. Roscov was still nervous, even though Hunter was treating him as if they had known each other forever.

Hunter introduced him to the bartender and the few customers he knew, who appeared to be somehow related to the world of literature or the arts. Hunter and Roscov ended up drinking scotch until late in the night, smoking cigars, and telling stories about their lives as if they were brothers-in-arms meeting by chance years after the end of the war.

Roscov was overwhelmed by how natural his conversation with Hunter turned out to be, by the unreserved trust the writer had in him, by the fact that he was being treated as an equal in the rarified field of literature. Hunter would ask for his opinions, would provoke him to comment on and analyze particular authors, books, or critical categories; he would correct or contradict Roscov only gently, like a teacher who wants to bring out the best in his favorite student.

But the most interesting moments were provided by Hunter's confessions about writing. Roscov was proud to have been elected to hear secrets about writing, creative states, feelings, quirks, and habits. It was so exciting to peek into a famous man's writing habits and motivations, to learn the backstage details of a kind of work usually surrounded by an ineffable cloud.

"I began to write too late. I was over forty when I published my first short story in *The New Yorker*. I had written only occasionally, for my own pleasure, until then. I was teaching at a college on Long

Island and was bored to death. I would read a lot, and it's very hard to get by only by reading. You start wanting to write. Have you ever felt this? Have you have felt that you, too, can do it, that you, too ,have something to say, to add?"

"No, I don't think so." Roscov hesitated.

"Not yet," Hunter corrected him, smiling in a slightly ironic way. "I can feel the writer in you."

Roscov's head spun for a second. He was both flattered and embarrassed by Hunter's suspicion.

"We keep being thrown traps. And we're happy to fall into them. After *The New Yorker* published me, I started to take myself seriously. My colleagues in the department were very impressed by my achievement. I felt it was my duty not to disappoint them. In fact, writing is just a way of satisfying one's ego. In the beginning, you write out of vanity. Then you write in order to flatter yourself. I don't discount passion in all this, but prose writing is hard labor. There's no pleasure in it. Some call it a talent or a gift. I think it's just about carrying out a task, a chore you are told to do. You fall ill with the duty to write, and everything else takes a back seat, as when you have to deal with a serious illness. Professional accolades are no longer important, even family becomes a secondary priority. In fact, in a way you write for them too. Or sometimes despite them, if you happen to have a needy wife or indifferent children. In the beginning, you're just trying to prove to yourself that you can do it. Afterwards, you can't stop. Of course, success and fame count for a lot in this whole affair. You are always within a short distance of arrogance or obsession. Every time you walk out there to get an award, failure is just around the corner. Fame can tickle your ego and drive you to all sorts of errors or compromises. It's like walking a tightrope. If your attention slips for even a fraction of a second, you find yourself lying flat on the ground. There are so many others who are at least as good as you that your fall might never get noticed. People note only success, no one has time for losers."

Roscov was looking at him with moist, admiring eyes.

"I am overwhelmed by the strength writers have, by...."

"You should be overwhelmed by their weakness, too. And besides, there's only one small step between being a reader and being a writer. Only a matter of courage. Some readers do dare to take up writing. That's all. Just write your first line. Dare yourself to write the first line. Everything else follows automatically. What about talent? Yes, one could talk about talent in the same terms as one could talk about luck: you can make your own. In fact, what people admire in the best of us is perseverance, the ambition of seeing things through, irrespective of circumstances or costs."

All of Hunter's conversations assumed some fundamental contradiction as their basis. One got the impression that the only reason he sought company was to argue. He always positioned his discourse by contradicting whomever he was speaking with.

He then launched into a long demonstration that amassed evidence that at times contradicted itself. It seemed as if this might be the only way he could communicate. Maybe he was a lonely man, Roscov thought, but then, how can a famous man like him be lonely?

"Most people write out of weakness or solitude. Those who write out of weakness are trying to provoke their destiny, to prove that they can overcome their complexes, and to show that they have a world all of their own, which only they can control with no interference from the outside world. The lonely ones write in order to squash their fears. There is something pathological about every great writer, a chemical imbalance, a degree of deviation from the norm. Loneliness is a good way to get into writing, whether the isolation is imposed or voluntary, traumatic or optional, real or imaginary. There are so many forms of loneliness, it's not hard to find one."

"Of course, metaphorically speaking, every writer is alone," Roscov attempted.

"Metaphorically like hell! Who do you think would want to live with a writer? Oh, it might be pleasant to be around one for a while, to sniff the glory and the fascination that surrounds him, but who do you think could last though to the end? Writers are impossible people. They are finicky, bizarre, hard to take in the long run. Some develop a persecution complex; others, on the other hand, can become enamored with themselves. They can be boring or, even worse, eccentric. Listen to me, I know what I'm talking about, I've seen a lot of things in my life, and sometimes I can even see myself as I really am. Tonight, I might be willing to risk my own life for you, but tomorrow I might pass you by without even a flicker of recognition."

Andrei Roscov looked at him askance.

"Well, that's just a manner of speaking." Hunter tried to mend things. "I mean that writers are unpredictable and that their reactions often follow a different logic from most people. They live in a disorderly universe created by themselves that has a hard time following the general rules of living. They like to pose so much that they fail to distinguish the model from the original, and they stop making an effort to avoid posing. They end up becoming histrionic and taking the shape of characters they themselves gave birth to."

Roscov was startled. Didn't he feel the same way, even as a mere reader? Maybe Hunter was right: what distinguished the reader from the writer was courage. Come to think of it, everything Hunter was telling him applied to him, too — he felt it, he lived it, even though he had never written a line in his life.

"Once, at one of these readings, I ran into this woman who went to junior high with me. She was living in Chicago but had come to New York with her husband for a few days. He was attending some medical convention of sorts. She had seen my name in an ad in the *Village Voice*, so she showed up at the bookstore to see me again, decades later. 'I'm surprised you're a writer,' she said, kindly. 'I'm surprised you're not,' I answered politely. I tried, unsuccessfully, to convince her that being a writer was a choice, that I hadn't just turned into a writer, that I had chosen to be one."

"If it were really so easy, the world would be swarming with writers," Roscov said.

"But it *is* that easy. And the world *is* actually swarming with writers. I'm not talking about the established ones or the ones who call themselves writers or aspire to be writers. I'm talking about those who don't write but could We each have in ourselves an infinite number of latent little people gifted in an infinite number of fields. We just don't let them out. We don't allow them to manifest themselves, that's a whole other story. But it's up to us. They continue to wait there, patiently, fully prepared to spread throughout the world. But we are afraid of our own infinite abilities and insist on keeping them locked up inside us, suffocated by our complexes and our cowardice and by the comfortable mediocrity that every day billions of people prove to be a viable way to make a living. It's against this complacency that that we must rise. Those who don't accept this insipid abandonment, the complacency in the general mud bath, are the special few, the trailblazers, the mold breakers, the destiny carvers, those who push the world forward. For them, everything is just a horrible, permanent chore, a perpetual discontentment, a painful never-ending birth. They spit out exceptional little people on a daily basis, and cater to their well-being in this world so eager to chew up exceptional little people."

Roscov swallowed air. He was touched, hurt, defeated. He almost saw inside himself an army of little people waiting, disappointed by their host's inability to spit them out. He felt small, helpless, and guilty. It wasn't enough that Jesus had planted words in his chest; now Hunter was at it with his little people.

Astonished at what he was discovering inside himself and unable to figure out what he was supposed to do, he fell prey to the endless glasses of scotch the bartender kept bringing as if Roscov were trying to wash away all the words and drown all the little people who were trying to turn his life upside down. Just when reading had brought him balance and peace, everything had begun to change again.

He could hardly wait to get home, open the first book he saw, and start reading. Reading would certainly give back the confidence, peace, and security he had worked so hard to achieve through organized, systematic, passionate, and responsible reading. This way he could free himself from the guilt and reproaches so cruelly thrust upon him.

His mother's face came to mind. Her eyes were scolding him even now. Was he reading too much for her taste? Was there anything more she expected of him?

Hunter was going through the shot glasses fast. His eyes had grown moist, he had begun to smack his lips, and a rivulet of saliva had formed at the corners of his mouth.

"Look around you. Only lonely little birds."

He was speaking slowly, dissecting the bar crowd with his eyes, stopping at various groups of huddled patrons. He was speaking mostly for himself, even though Roscov continued to listen to him attentively, hanging on his every word.

"The consequence of all this madness with sexual harassment: all poetry went to hell. What's the use of some of them being smart, others talented, and others successful? They all reek of ambition; they are merciless and sure of themselves, the macho kind — you know, they have money, they are accomplished, and they wouldn't renounce anything for the sake of a man. Now that they have gotten even the rights they didn't need, now that they have become superior to us, now that they're encouraged by this politically correct society, we're not worth much in their eyes. Whatever we do, they can do, too. Whatever we have, they can have, too. They satisfy themselves — or each other. Oh, where are the love intrigues of yesteryear! Where is the suffering, the depression, the mad passion, the sacrifice, the suicides of unfulfilled lovers?"

Hunter issued a melancholy hiccup.

"We are going headlong towards violent and promiscuous matriarchy. Just think about all the sidewalks with toned legs in silk stockings and sneakers, running all over the place all day long, energetic and competitive. How horrid! In fact, it's quite sad, even for them, no matter how hard they're trying to play the champions. You know, I don't believe the easy-going air they put on when they choose solitude. In fact, none of these beer-drinking broads giggling to each other and casting glances at the lonely men at the tables is truly happy. They yearn for a real male who can drive them out of their minds. But they're proud and the men are timid, full of complexes, defeated before the race. Many men were castrated by this idea of sexual harassment! Sometimes I miss Europe so dearly, our old-fashioned granny with runs in her stockings, with black-and-white photo albums and run-down walls. At least there you can pinch a woman's butt in the street without ending up in court. And women smell like women over there! And they can sniff a man from a distance, too. They let themselves be picked up, they expect manipulation and seduction. I so miss some European booty! What if we went to Paris on a lark? Or to Rome! Will you come to Rome with me?"

But he didn't wait for the answer, which Roscov was trying to make as evasive as possible so as not to ruin Hunter's mood.

"Our generation saw the death of the family. The generation right after ours dismantled the couple — what with feminism, on the one hand, AIDS, on the other hand, let alone alienation, egotism, survival."

"Are you married?" Roscov asked.

"I was. Three times. And all of the marriages were successful," grinned Hunter, his eyes still moist with the image of Europe, which was slowly fading in the last scotch glass downed under the admiring eyes of the bartender, who kept Hunter's photo on the wall alongside those of a few other famous patrons such us Paul Simon and Hillary Clinton.

They wobbled into the street. Hunter hailed a cab. Instead of sobering them up, the cold wind rocked the two men ridiculously. Their cheeks burned and their eyes turned red. Each had other reasons besides alcohol for their behavior.

"Now what?" Hunter asked, balancing himself against the cab's door. "We're not gonna go home, are we?!"

Roscov's white scarf was fluttering like a symbol of surrender. It was past midnight.

"I live far upstate. I have to go to work tomorrow.'

"Aaah! That's right. You have a job. What do you care about a writer's insomnia!'

The cab driver motioned impatiently. Now Roscov was supposed to feel guilty for having a job, for not being an insomniac?!

"All right...but I'll see you tomorrow night at my place. 26 Green Street. The top buzzer."

Hunter fought his way into the cab, folding his coat. Roscov was left in the street. His arm lifted to hail the next cab, his chest laid waste by a pain never experienced before.

He found his wife awake and worried. He had never come home so late. He used to rush home as fast as he could, so he could start reading.

"I was afraid something happened to you. Are you all right? Where have you been all this time?"

"In a bar."

"A baaar?!" his wife cried indignantly. "You, in a bar?"

"With Allen Hunter."

"The writer?"

"You know him?"

"Who doesn't? He's in the newspapers all day long, he's on TV, in shop windows. Oh my God, you and Hunter?"

"What?! Why not? Me and Hunter."

"Where did you meet him? And how did you get to..."

"Friends. We became friends. We have a lot of things in common. And then there are the grandmothers, both from Bukovina."

The look on his wife's face mixed distrust, irony, admiration, and jealousy.

"Oh yeah?"

"I'm seeing him again tomorrow night."

"Oh yeah?"

"What's with you?"

"Nothing, nothing. I was thinking that you started to have a personal life. Can I come along?"

"I don't think so. Not yet. And I think you'd get bored...We talk about all sorts of technical stuff, so to speak."

"Such as...?"

"Creating, writing, people, little people..." Roscov stammered.

"Oh, so you've become intimate," the wife took a stab at him. "Maybe you think I couldn't sustain this kind of conversation, since I don't have your extensive readings..."

"Ella, I'm tired. Can we continue this tomorrow? I have to get up at seven for work."

"You're still going to work after hobnobbing with Hunter?"

"OK, OK, I get it that you're angry."

"I'm not angry, I'm bewildered."

"All right, you'll get used to the idea. I have to go to bed."

"Aren't you going to read?"

"Now? No way, I'm exhausted."

"Then let's go to sleep together."

"Now?!"

"I said go to sleep, I had no other intentions."

"OK, let's go to bed — but you know I'll be snoring. I drank a lot and I'm beat."

"It's all right. You can snore. I'll use earplugs."

Roscov looked at her gratefully.

"Was it really Allen Hunter? Himself?"

"Stop it, Ella. It was him."

They fell asleep in each other's arms, with the smell of alcohol and Hunter's ghost floating above their bed.

The next night, eight o'clock sharp, Roscov pressed the top buzzer at 26 Green Street. He was holding a bottle of scotch. His long white scarf had been replaced by a one that was dark blue. He rang a couple of times with no response. He stood about five minutes in front of the building, ringing the buzzer a couple dozen times. It looked as if Hunter had forgotten about him. He wasn't home.

Disappointed and a bit humiliated, Roscov walked away slowly, aimlessly. He walked into the first bar, ordered a scotch, and began to feel ridiculous. He regretted not having a book to read while sipping his drink watered down with ice.

Whenever he was tense, stressed out, or just tired, Roscov resorted to a relaxation method he had learned from an immigrant healer from Kiev, the kind of transcendental therapist who was always moving between paranormal aptitudes and convincing impostures.

During a few friendly sessions, Igor, the healer, had taught him to stay in control in moments of crisis, to dig back into his memory and face the traumas of his past in order to free himself from emotions and obsessions, to concentrate on a particular point on the wall in front of him and imagine soothing colors. Above all, the healer had taught Roscov visualization.

Even if he were always afraid to relive shameful, painful, or humiliating memories, he was fascinated by visualization. Once he had reached such an advanced stage that he was able to relive his childhood with its smell of burnt milk, its brighter colors, stronger tastes, and more terrifying heights, with the small accidents that appeared catastrophic, with catastrophes passing him by without being understood, with strange adults and devastating curiosity. Sometimes he was even able to remember things he had not experienced.

He could see vast milky fields through which his mother, herself a child, would run barefoot in a fluttering little dress, gathering flowers and singing in the thin voice of an angel run aground on earth. He would calm down, his breath would become shallow and regular, and a sort of weightlessness would take hold of his muscles and joints. He would experience the floating sensation he imagined astronauts knew. He would close his eyes, letting his arms hang down as if he were a discarded puppet. He would experience bright colors springing from his forehead like paint spilling from a bucket. This was a simple trick he could perform on the subway, at work, at the theater, in the park.

Igor had taught him to enter a state of deep relaxation by imagining a sphere of light practically anywhere. Thus Roscov, still in the bar where he was recovering from being stood up by Hunter, closed his eyes and tried to empty his mind of thoughts, just as Igor had taught him. This was the hardest part — emptying one's mind of thoughts. He could hear Hunter insisting, "Art is something optional. You either resort to it or not, you either need it or not, you either decide to dedicate your time to it or decide to do something else instead. In fact, art does not need an audience. It's an ethereal gesture, meant for an abstract eternity. Books don't even need to be read. But they do need to be written."

Then Hunter's words took on a metallic tone in Roscov's head: "You could be a very good writer. You are a skilled listener. That's the first sign. If you like listening to others, if you have the strength to listen to others. Then comes a stage when you begin to write in your head. You write tens, hundreds of pages in your mind. Putting that stuff down on paper is peanuts. I wrote my best pages all in my head. God only knows how few of them ended up transcribed on paper!"

Roscov saw the sphere of light above his head and slowly lowered it onto his forehead, then let it slide down his neck, caressing his thyroid, down his chest, feeling it slowly crawl along his stomach and then, very slowly, down to his toes. He lifted it just as slowly all the way up to the top of his head. The sphere left behind a trail pleasantly warm.

Roscov relaxed and calmed down until, having reached the top of his head, the sphere exploded, and a shining light invaded his body, giving him so much energy that his body, now strong and fully recovered, was shaken by a powerful wave of emotion.

He opened his eyes. The bartender was studying him, worried that he might be on drugs or about to have a heart attack. Roscov smiled back strategically, finished his scotch, paid, and left, his dark blue scarf billowing in the air. He passed Hunter's house again but did not give in to the impulse to ring the buzzer again.

When he reached home, the hand in which he had been clutching the bottle of scotch was asleep. Ella was waiting in the hallway among books that had taken refuge from the rooms in which others were stacked.

"Well, how was it?"

Roscov averted his eyes.

"All right."

"All right? What's that? I was expecting superlatives. Tell me more."

She wet her lips, opened her eyes wide, leaned against the dining room door, ready to hang on her husband's every word.

"He wasn't home. Maybe, I don't know, something came up..."

"He wasn't home? You mean, this whole story about Allen Hunter was made up? You flexed your imagination at my expense?" Ella shouted, grinning maliciously. She hesitated between continuing to humiliate him or being compassionate

"You're either naïve, or a liar, or a sucker. Or perhaps you're having an affair..."

"Stop it. I'm not having an affair. He just wasn't home. I rang the intercom like crazy. Maybe he forgot."

"Ha! I should have expected it. Nonsense, this whole thing about you being friends with Hunter! Just like that! All the confessions, the invitations to spend time at his place... Nonsense! I've suffered though your reading mania, but I'm not going to take this! Are you very sure this whole thing is not about another woman?"

"I'm sure," Roscov mumbled. "I'm going to take a shower."

"Take two!"

Ella went back to the bedroom, slamming the door behind her.

That night Roscov went to bed earlier than usual. Once more, exhaustion overcame him, together with the dissatisfaction of his failure. Not a very consequential failure but an irritating one, one that bothered his enflamed ego.

He chose a book, opened it, and tried to lose himself in it. He tried to return to certitudes, to that part of his life that he could control, to that part of his life where no one was going to slam a door in his face. But his eyes began to sting after only a few pages. A tear rolled down his cheek. It must be exhaustion, he thought. He turned off the light and squeezed his eyelids tight until those tiny points of light he knew so well from his childhood reappeared.

What if there were something wrong with his eyes? What if he was about to go blind? The very idea of darkness and especially the thought that he might have to give up reading terrified him. They were going to take his books away from him. An endless night would take hold of his soul and mind. Was the radiating pencil of light in his dream a providential sign? Or maybe just ironic?

He could see himself useless and powerless with all those words boiling in his chest, with all his potential destinies unfulfilled. He remembered that once in a museum he had seen a gallery for the blind. There was a large room where copies of famous Roman and Greek sculptures were placed so that the blind could touch them and imagine what art looked like. He had found himself there by mistake while looking for the Impressionist rooms, lost in the gigantic maze of the museum.

Only two men with dark glasses were in the gallery. They had let their white canes fall to the floor. They both wore white raincoats, which fluttered on their frail bodies. They were feeling the cold marble, embracing the statues, caressing the ample shapes in silence. The scene looked like a pantomime, like a ballet without music, beautiful and sad.

Roscov relived the scene with some envy. At least the blind could feel the art. He, on the other hand, might never be able to read. He turned the light on, startled. He looked around. The objects were all where they should be, but he continued to feel his eyes stinging.

It had to be something temporary and unimportant. Roscov consoled himself, trying to escape his fantasy about losing his sight. He opened his book again and went back to reading. Words were there, like little people ready to take over the world.

ESSAYS
FLESH OF WORDS

IN SEARCH OF THE ESSENCE

In my childhood I would choose a word and repeat it over and over until it lost its meaning. The syllables would pile up, one on another and sound like a language not yet invented or long abandoned, something mysterious and antique, rough and absurd. The vowels would lose their clarity. Instead of opening up and reverberating, their sounds would be smothered. Crushed like hands caught between heavy metal doors, they would be shattered and dismembered and crash on top of the consonants, stubbornly trying to maintain a rhythm. I was fascinated by the battle of letters against sounds, unable to represent or sustain themselves anymore. The word would then become tangible, heavy, like a hunk of clay tossed into the ocean. I would await its dissolution and watch for its disappearance while continuing to repeat it, compulsively, like a juvenile delinquent unable to contain the joy felt in her crime.

The sounds would come unglued one by one: fleshy petals with nails and blood or star dust, floating in the air until they stuck randomly to the ceiling or the floor, to a chair or to my dress. My dress was covered with bits and pieces of words — short vowels with slashed throats, stubby syllables, arrogant letters, mountain crests and a mishmash of tangled algae. Here a touch of orange in cloudy water, there a rainbow fallen into a puddle. Square consonants or angled corners, diaphanous cut-outs. I would repeat a word until its flesh was completely stripped off, until only a white, frail bone was left, a demented and futile phalange pointing to the sky.

What are words? Are they energy, matter, or ineffable beings? Where do they come from and where are they heading? I wondered, looking at my dress, which kept traces of them in its light fabric.

I felt the same perplexities about myself. I would sit on the edge of my bed and move my arms, listening to my heart beating, I stared at my feet on the rug. I could even see the blood running through my veins. My body seemed to separate from myself, leaving room for me to see it as if it were an illusory wrapping. I would extend my hand outward in order to touch my body to make sure it still existed. Reality. Shape. Chaos starting beyond the edge of my bed like a dark abyss down which I could plunge at any time. What was all this for, what was expected of me? And what was I expecting from those words given to me, surely not just that I would be obsessively twisting their necks?

This is how my adventure and interest in the essence of words started: on a winter morning, crushing ice under my heavy boots, and repeating *snow, snow, snow...* until the entire city became first a blue globe, then a thin, tingling thread, only to end up as a melted ethereal flake, a white molecule that, to this day, is traveling from one life to another, from one universe to the next.

All this was on my mind as I was sitting on the edge of the bed, not understanding why my left arm was moving up, what I was made of, where the tears came from and where the floor ended, still repeating the word *WORD*, until a door slammed somewhere, causing the startled letters to jump back into place. Order. Measure. Time.

❧

In the long run, a respect for words is what separates us from one another. In my adolescence I became intuitively aware of the gravity of words. One night I even got so far as to dream of them. They were buried at the root of an imposing tree. I was digging with my bare hands, deeper into the guts of Earth, my hands burning and blood gushing from beneath my nails; I was pulling weeds, crushing ants and bugs, feverishly searching, perspiring in anticipation, and suddenly, here they were: one by one, perfectly contoured, neat concrete shapes, nothing abstract or incomprehensible about them. Round stones, like Japanese crystals polished by water, scalloped shells, spiral-boned horns, drops of frozen ink, breathtakingly beautiful frescoes as if torn from a magnificent temple buried at the root of that tree, so that they would be kept hidden, to be uncovered and given to those searching for their essence.

I placed each of them in my palm, carefully cleaned the dirt away, and, as I was blowing over them to dissipate the last trace of dust, they became lighter, took airy shapes and flew about me in milky white circles, and then, more and more transparent, they burst like bubbles and disappeared beyond the horizon, but not before each pirouetted, touching my forehead. It was a long and very realistic dream, which I had to interrupt several times to calm down the outpouring of rebellious words that kept circling, braided together, incapable of separating from one another.

I woke up with a heavy head. Light flooded the room, and instantly I forgot everything. But just glancing at my hands, which still hurt, I remembered them digging in the dirt at the root of the tree.

෨

You may sometimes dream your faith on solstice nights, or after long stretches of meditation and spiritual initiation, or simply when the turmoil of searching becomes unbearable. At that time, I had no inkling that I would become a writer. I was studying mathematics, which I gladly would have changed for directing plays, but the communist Eastern European world where I lived did not encourage dreams.

The words imposed by the dictatorship would take up a mere two dictionary pages: empty slogans, political clichés, tortured syntagma emptied of meaning. We lived a linguistic nightmare from which all who could escape did.

Artists would hide behind metaphors; ordinary people would murmur and curse. Some would make peace with the system and become megaphones of ideological emptiness; others would assume the loneliness of their own thoughts awaiting, more and more hopelessly, a liberating miracle.

We lived a double life, each in a different language. We talked in a certain way in public or when being watched, and in another way among ourselves. Paradoxically, we were still *communicating*. Through that communication, we were surviving culturally and keeping mind and soul sane. Language had become a living animal that would insidiously squeeze inside our walls and penetrated the design of our rugs. It flew — simulating freedom — from one window to the next, condensed, profound, intense, and alert, and we cherished each word as a hidden treasure.

What could be easier than talk; what is more natural than rolling words about your mouth? Nevertheless, we had become aware that what was normal for those beyond the Iron Curtain was resistance to us. We were stealing words and carefully protecting their mystery and sanity. We couldn't afford to cheapen them, nor could we let them emerge at random. We each had only one life to live, and the obsession to leave something true and authentic behind.

Paradoxically, after the fall of the Berlin Wall when the live animal was freed from the cage that had imprisoned him for decades, language woke up confused and disoriented. It sprang up unchained and unclear, sniffing the new reality, adjusting its steps and making unnatural leaps over abysses and lost history. The faucet was fully open, the fences torn down, the barbed wire broken.

But the newly found freedom was difficult, and too few knew how to live in it. It was here to stay with all its fears and uncertainties, with the wild roaming of the language free of official control. Some started to swim though afraid of water, some learned to fly though afraid of heights, others started to imitate the western world we had so much longed for, swallowing its rules automatically, randomly, without chewing, wishing only to catch up and be like them.

Language, kept for so long in the dowry chest and suddenly free, lost its core and often its beauty as well. Communication became pragmatic and efficient for some, trivial for others. Now there was need for a different resistance on another esthetic level, to avoid falling into another noisy inferno of emptiness, this time the emptiness of consumer society.

It seemed to me that the challenge in being a writer was inspiring, the perfect theater where the grace and pleasure of handling words and preserving their meaning.

The roots of the tree would go deeper and deeper into the soft soil of my dreams; they would reach far into the guts of the earth, hiding small shiny rocks, traces of clouds, blue and purple molecules in which life was endlessly resurrected. You only had to dig, push the soil away.

REVEALING METAPHORS
OR COMMON VERBS

When I came to America I felt like Columbus. I had been conquered and I was, in turn, conquering. New York was the right place for immersion in my new life. I started by liking it all — the white chairs in Bryant Park, the fire escapes in Soho, the squirrels and the dancer known as Thoth in Central Park, the mayor, the steel and the glass, the flags around the Rockefeller Center skating rink, the champagne drunk during intermission at the Met Opera while gazing over the fountain at Lincoln Center to the Fiorello Restaurant and the art cinema across the street, the subway entrances and grates from which warm steam and a stale smell of crumpled cardboard rose in the winter, the sirens of police cars and the lugubrious yelp of fire trucks, the yellow cabs, and the ceiling of Grand Central Station where artificial stars shone in turquoise circles during the holidays, the vibration of asphalt under streets girded with bodies rushing with cell phones hanging from their ears, the purple nails and gold clinking bracelets of supermarket cashiers, the extravagant shop windows in the Village and the factories turned into art galleries in Soho. I was in love with everything, without discrimination, with the joy of beginning and a feeling of being the 'chosen' one, and therefore allowed to love generically.

For almost two years I devoted myself to discovery. I couldn't write anything but enthusiastic articles that glorified the new world in which I was learning to live and that were published in journals in my native country, where everyone had figured out I wasn't coming back.

I had arrived in New York as a diplomat, the director of cultural programs at the Romanian Cultural Center. The city possessed me at first sight, and although crushed under its energy, I was following its lead as in a trance from which I didn't want to emerge. My imagination already had built a place of my own in its engulfing belly.

After a while I calmed down and started to look closer. By then, I had willingly anchored myself to the millstone, turning rhythmically with everyone else, my social security card sheltered in a closed drawer. I opened my eyes and pricked up my ears as if awakening in a strange place after the party was over, the lights turned off, and the last guest having closed the door behind himself.

As a new immigrant, I didn't feel displaced, neither was I experiencing identity crises or nostalgia. All my senses were intensely awake and alive *here*.

I was pulling my new life over my head like a shirt that I knew would fit since I had carefully tailored it. At least I did not let myself be disappointed by dreams that ended differently from what I wished. This time, from inside the whale's belly, I had found comfort that I started to explore.

❧

When you land from a different culture, you can uninhibitedly observe from a distance the world you are supposed to enter. By comparing and weighing nuances and differences, specifics and similarities, you can place yourself in a favorable situation freely chosen, that of a referee who wants to prevent errors and unnecessary penalties, blowing his whistle only when the game becomes chaotic. What happens to you in the scenario you have created really matters, whether the usual spectators are passive or alert, or if they are much too used to the routine and rules of the game.

For more than thirty years I lived in the opaque world of communism, where time meant nothing. In the absence of any real dialogue within its social and political structures, all we had was talking among ourselves. In that Balkan atmosphere, our conversations, sometimes brilliantly lit by life in a ruined "little Paris," as Bucharest was known, were delightful, baroque, a never-ending chatter, spectacular and useless, over full ashtrays and cheap alcohol, night-long discussions and hung-over mornings when it would start all over again. We weren't in a hurry to get anywhere. We had no place to go.

The dictatorship seemed permanent. To keep our sanity we only had words, the language, airy imaginative phantasms, grim existential critiques, fable-making, hair-splitting. Bright ideas or dashing banalities. Survival. Words were powerless to change our destiny, but they were therapeutic in keeping us sane. The Soul? No one mentioned it, but it was there all along in the arabesques of our lamentations, in the last cigarette butt crushed at sunrise on a background of a hideous smoking factory on the outskirts of the city.

Time is everything in America. It is sold at each Deli and hot-dog cart, on TV and by insurance companies, on slot-machines and with Staten Island ferry tickets, in the *Have a nice day* greeting everyone utters automatically, sometimes, to get rid of you quickly. Using concentrated formulas of conventional language does not stem from emptiness, but from fear of lingering too long in a syntagma which is not likely to bring anything new when weighed against *Have a nice day! Time is money.* The Soul? It is lying somewhere on a shrink's couch or in TV talk shows.

From inside the belly of the whale, I quickly sketched the steps of loneliness: from *chosen* isolation, where you have the revelation of your own interior beauty, to *imposed* solitude, where you look up to the tops of the buildings and don't see the stars; from *seclusion,* where a good book keeps you warm, to *estrangement,* where the language becomes powerless, and further, to *alienation,* where words lose their meanings and weight. The essence of communication slips into the ridiculous, not out of emptiness, but from fear of doing something forbidden, lingering on a syllable, rolling around the word *love* until your chest is pumped up and your nostrils dilate, a page from Henry Miller stays with you, and you actually feel love piercing you with scents and tactile sensations. Isn't it easier to watch *Sex and the City* or *Dr. Phil,* who has a solution for everything?

About Love

When I fell in love in my adolescence I didn't dare to utter the word *love* from fear that its magic would disappear. It was my secret, my hidden treasure. Our approach back then was to protect the word itself from public scrutiny. Was this cautious attitude part of our inhibitions inside a dictatorship or just a way to live one of the most powerful words?

In America *love* seems to be overused. Over here everyone loves from dawn to dusk, and no one is shy about publicly showing his or her love. Before hanging up the phone, after speaking with a friend, automatically out comes "love you," actually meaning something like "talk to you soon" or "good bye, farewell." Love extends to objects, dishes, landscapes and situations. People often say, *Oh, my God, I love this, I love that....* without nuance, ignoring synonyms such as *like, value, admire, appreciate, cherish, be attracted by,* etc. — words that offer differences in intensity and emotions. And while saying a few times a day *I love...* the mouth fills up with the vowel *o,* the word disappears, its weight is cancelled, the meaning lost.

Love repeated carelessly and continuously becomes all but worthless. At that point, Tolstoy might change his mind about having Karenina throw herself in front of a moving train. Instead he could send her to a shrink and launch into a tirade on the harmony of *mind, body, and soul* in search of the *interior child.*

I can remember how difficult it was to articulate *love* in my adolescence, the crazy pirouettes taken by our sentences, the way we weighed their intensity, graded their emotion, using an entire linguistically allusive arsenal. We were convinced that our inhibitions were due to education and that it would be indecent to dispel the mystery and force of the strongest word by saying it randomly, or that having said it, we would wake up exposed and vulnerable, or we would strike sentimental chords. And what if, once uttered, the word *love* hit a wall? Of all humiliations, ridicule is the worst. Furthermore, we lived in a closed society where discussing sex was taboo, contraception was interdicted, and love was confounded by the communist ideologues with either the party or reproduction. I feel as if all this happened a hundred years ago...

How easy it is today to deal with love as sex, although a huge gap separates the sexes in big American cities, where having a career and/or being single is highly regarded. At the end of the day, liberated women and successful men, castrated by a fear of sexual harassment, hunt each other in bars, laughing over cocktails and beer, exhausted from harrowing workdays. Their talk is often strident. What one says doesn't matter; what is important is to be heard, giving an impression of being detached, sufficient, self-confident inside a politically correct society. And men and women will start this game of flirting all over again the next day.

If you look closer and put your ear next to the words, machine-gunned from one to the other under the pressures of communication, the impression of a universal loneliness can be overwhelming, Only the surface motivations shine.

A couple's relationship is marked by estrangement, oscillating between contact and competition. A game of ego and youthful rivalry dominated by a struggle to establish supremacy (in bed, in children's education, in decision making) turns into a boring and dusty relationship in later years where each will count the other's errors while considering him- or herself blameless. They each carry, unspoken, the status of the victim. Authentic communication, avoided for years, delayed and compromised, doesn't have the strength to establish itself fully or save anything.

The partners know their duties inside the family regarding children, but each feels frustrated because of not getting attention, not being listened to, pitied, or admired as much as he or she feels is deserved. Emotion and affection are filtered through formal communication where civility and correctness take center stage, leaving anger behind. The partners respect each other, or pretend to, omitting natural communication, authentic, uncensored, which could free them and draw them closer, creating an intimate space where private codes function.

In the absence of authentic communication, each partner says only what is allowed and doesn't dare to touch painful subjects or topics which they are uncomfortable. They repress their feelings. Unspoken words, inhibitions, and frustrations multiply and deeply damage the relationship. They keep saying *love you* at the end of a phone call but *love* is reduced to sterile reflexive language, incapable of sustaining its meaning. *To love* becomes a common verb, said without any special emotion, an expired ingredient random among ordinary recipes, without any flavor.

About Happiness

Happiness is another abused word. The entire nation is chasing after it, which wouldn't be absurd except that many pretend to find it several times a day in the most unexpected situations. Here, people do not seem to experience moderate joy, contentment, minor satisfactions. Instead, when something is just OK or funny, they appear happy.

A heavily weighted word, filled with magic, *happiness* should make you feel as if you had wings. To answer the question, "What was the happiest moment in your life?" people often sit and ponder for a while to choose the most intense experience. For a moment, they are responsible for the power of the word. However, in this quick-paced daily life, ordinary speech gives in to pretense and bravado, displaying a self-imposed optimism.

What is called *happiness* oscillates between *being entertainment, having fun, and enjoying* — palliatives to convince one that life is worth living. The vocabulary associated with this ambition is marked by superlatives and exaggerations to support *enthusiasm*.

On Broadway, humor is pursued in every word and gesture. Although I was fond of American comedies in the '70s and '80's, today I can hardly find authentic humor in American theater, film or television. More discordant is the spectator's laughter. He is looking for fun no matter where. In today's entertainment from cartoons to stand-up comedy, one finds a dose of hysteria fueled by the desperate need of marketing in an environment more and more anxiously searching for cultural milestones, or, rather, for the lack thereof.

In spite of happiness, obsessively sought through wealth or the comforts possible inside a well-regulated system, there is much sorrow, grief, and poverty in America. Sometimes poverty and sadness rise to the surface like tragic alarms. Devastating images were brought to light by the muddy waters that swallowed New Orleans following hurricane Katrina: another America, not the picture-perfect one, but the one hidden in silence, projecting an uncomfortable image in contradiction to the values of the American dream — a dream more and more pragmatic, without poetry or idealism, but designed to make a profit.

About Optimism and Fatalism

All languages have routine expressions that characterize the mentality of the people at a given point. For example, in the country I come from, speech often operates though diminutives: *tarisoara*, little-country; *ciorbita*, little-soup; *pupic*, small kiss... signifying a familiarity of communication and intimacy, but also the vulgarization of the language as spoken by ordinary people who want to be funny, ironic, or humble.

In America, however, the hyperbolic rules, serving a need for grandiosity; everything is oversized.

At first, that positive American spirit energized me. Coming from a fatalistic Romanian mentality, I found instead an optimistic, serene approach: *don't worry, be happy*, or, in other words, *there is always room for something better.*

I enjoyed the frankness of my new friends and casual acquaintances, asking naïve and sincere questions without any knowledge of my country and the dictatorship I had lived under. Many knew about Dracula, very few about Romanian culture, but they wanted to learn; they would listen to my stories in profound and honest astonishment, and I felt encouraged by their warm welcome.

My first month in New York I was touched by *how are you*, a salutation more than a question, used by everybody, friends and strangers, to greet me everywhere — not to mention the most wonderful and warm expression that broke my heart each time: "Take care!" I could have developed a certain vanity driven by the feeling that everybody wanted to find out how I was doing, caring about me. But before I could answer, my companion was gone — *time is money* — displaying the same open smile as everyone else in New York, a smile full of white teeth and apparent optimism.

In my country, I was fed up with the eternal lamentations of people on every topic. They would complain any time they had a chance. They felt almost guilty doing well and were embarrassed to admit it. If you praised them, you would be contradicted with extensive explanations of how looks can be deceiving. In fact, it went without saying that they were not doing well at all.... They wished to be miserable, pitied.

A New Yorker, even one with a foot in the grave, when asked how he is doing, will calmly answer *thank you, I am fine, great, OK*, and the answer, beyond its formality, implicitly means he is not sharing his problems or uneasiness with you. For an outsider it looks as if this sparse formal language produces alienation, seclusion, and superficial relationships. However, for an American it can be the result of common decency and a desire not to burden others with his or her problems.

On the other hand, the excess of strong words — *love, happiness,* etc. — is a pretext for avoiding living profoundly. Speech is used in reverse, not to be open and communicative, but to hide and protect oneself, an isolation imposed by standardization.

As I began to understand the spirit of the place, I felt like placing in quarantine depreciated and tired words, clichés replacing specifics, standardization choking refreshingly enigmatic and essential insights.

Left to their own devices, living their full intensity and depth, words would overturn order and derail society. It's no surprise then that official speech is primarily meant to erase subliminally from the subconscious any metaphysics or philosophy. How can anyone possibly breathe in a word and fill up on its significance in a world of mass media, skillful politicians, overwhelming commercials, evangelical preachers? They all tell you exactly what you should feel and how you should think. But you believe them at your peril.

Communication is overseen by other rationales: efficiency, competition, and leadership. It is patriotic to stay on the surface of the words. It is for your own good to opt for superficial dialogue. There is no time either to split hairs or to choose surreal fantasies that could derail and mislead you spiritually from the standardized society. Swimming against the tide is not encouraged.

I have been writing these thoughts during the holiday season.

On CNN an anchorwoman happily informs us about the latest scientific findings that show that shopping is therapeutic, cures neurotic behavior, and lessens depression, can even make you happy, especially if you pay with cash and not with credit cards. She interviews a psychiatrist, a distinguished academic who confirms the benefits of shopping for a soul adrift. Her piece ends with the words of an old man sharing his happiness roaming the shopping malls and buying indiscriminately. He gives a quirky smile that could express happiness, irony, or simply neurosis.

About Old Age and Death

There also are painful topics: old age and death are regarded as signs that one has been defeated. And the reason is not difficult to find in a civilization of champions who have no time to waste, who see themselves as colonizers of values, to whom Mars seems closer than Europe, and whose political leaders believe they have a direct line to God. It is humiliating to die when you should be among the strong, at a time when you should be enjoying personal, national, and interplanetary conquests.

It is true that significant progress has been made in health and longevity, possibly out of fear, vanity, or ambition. Similarly, an entire industry guaranteeing everlasting youth has been perfected based on denying old age and death.

I remember how shocked I was when, a few moths after I arrived in New York, I discovered several religious programs on TV where thousands of people were listening to ministers, pastors, and evangelists who taught them how to interpret the divine "word," how to deal with critical issues and find solutions to their problems. I knew that more Americans believe in God and go to church regularly than in any other country in the world, but I couldn't imagine the impact of these skilful orators who can electrify huge crowds. A friend explained, "It could be surprising for a foreigner, but it's nothing wrong. These people are not fanatics, just regular folks, kind and generous, with a desire to optimize their lives." Still, these people amazed me — something that my undisciplined, ironic, noisy, suspicious people back home would never be able to do!

In American society, obsessed with appearances, concerns about the body surpass spiritual training. This thrives in spite of a vast esoteric literature, mixing Asian concepts with diets and practical guides to prolong youth and delay death. The desperation not to die can also extend from clinics run by experts who pretend to have the secrets of immortality to attempts to break the genome code.

Today we are fighting to survive in a materialistic culture that has transformed religion into a profitable business and derailed its metaphors into commercials. When death is seen as an interruption and not as a matter of transformation and becoming, truth vanishes.

On Authority

Americans believe in, and submit to, authority. They are disciplined and obedient, and perhaps this is even the key to the system's strength. Their candor is backed up by trust and a sense of fairness, which contributes to the image, a cliché in itself, of a nation of childish and naïve people. That's exactly what surprised me from the day I arrived here. They looked open, friendly, and reliable, without prejudices, with large smiles and luminous faces. I had the feeling that we can communicate easily, and I was right. I felt safe and protected, because I trusted the people and their institutions.

I came from a world of suspicion and intrigue where each word was questioned from morning until night. We were always on watch for the lie or the trap laid for us. We didn't trust official institutions or our neighbors or coworkers. Anyone could rat on you or cheat you. If the evening news told you that the next day would be sunny, it was a good idea to take your umbrella. While the entire mass-media proclaimed the unprecedented accomplishments of communist society, it was obvious we were sinking deeper into obscurity and poverty.

Often we would try an experiment that seemed almost logical in an absurd and phony world: we would read official news in reverse, changing the affirmative into the negative, acting the opposite to any directive. We were responding to a life spent in a deep, narrow basement, a catacomb where one had to walk bent over, looking over one's shoulder to avoid dirty water dripping from the ceiling.

That's why I so appreciated the height and open spaces of New York. From the basement I sprang to the top floors. Even reaching up with my arm stretched, it seemed as if the ceiling were a mile away. Sometimes I would receive an email from my native country; I continued to publish there, proud of being a New Yorker. "How can you live in that virtual city, where the sky is never seen?" What my friend saw as 'virtual' had a real dimension for me. I didn't have a problem with the sky since I would imagine planes as birds in the day or as stars at night, and for that matter, didn't think the sky need always be above. Why couldn't it be anywhere I wanted it to be?

On the morning of September 11, 2001, I was listening to the radio when the broadcast was interrupted by the trembling voice of an announcer who broke in to say, "America is under attack." As happens when you get terrible news, you lose touch with reality and need to check whether you are awake.

The unconscious question, "What is to be done?" can stretch emotion in any direction from panic to hysteria. The city stuck to my soul, I felt the tragedy as a personal drama, a physical pain, and an endless humiliation. The connection between me and this place was set in stone. That morning an umbilical cord grew between me and the belly of the whale.

In 1989 I witnessed a revolution in my country, a bloody farce through which communism collapsed. A few years later it was a trick of destiny to be here in the most powerful fortress of freedom and see its towers collapse, but the ironies did not stop there. That morning was when the 21st century started, a time of radicalization of religious conflicts and desperate actions in many parts of the globe. The future swallowed the present. And we began living in the future with time accelerating to the maximum.

A tragedy can change people for the better, can purify the spirit of a place that has made a sacrifice. Everything you have hoped for a long time now happens instantly, a compensation for misfortune, a re-alignment of energies. In those days the routine was broken, people discovered deep meanings in existence and their ability to communicate profoundly. They were strong because they accepted their vulnerability. Everything was intense and unaltered by dissimulation, superficiality, or bravado. Words, gestures, silences had weight.

In the void a calamity leaves behind, things resume their dimensions uncensored by the imagination or the rigidities imposed by the culture. Everything is clear and sharp. The fog that clouds the everyday contact we have with reality lifts, and the initial structure springs out with beauty and primal simplicity. At that point there are moments of grace, when we find strength to return to ourselves, genuine.

A return to the normal becomes the goal, not redefining essential things but simply picking up where you left off. Communication maintains its conventions; the strong become more authoritarian, the weak more frail. History shows that times following disasters are fertile for dictatorships.

Since I lived for many years in a totalitarian society that capitalized on fears and intensified our weaknesses, my senses are alert to subdued or concealed forms of control, domination, and supremacy, especially when they justify themselves with words like *freedom* and *democracy*, or with imperatives like national security and the fight against terrorism.

The official discourse goes over the top, calling on patriotism, responsibility, and nationalism. Power claims religion in support of political measures. Everything is smooth, tacit, apparently unobtrusive, dissimulated by seemingly benevolent intentions.

The 21st century looks quite unpredictable with powerful leaders planning the future in their offices far from realities while ignoring criticism from the international arena. Analysts wring their hands, artists sharpen their pencils, and cynics laugh.

BE AWARE OF WORDS!

I was asked to recite a poem at a graduation ceremony at an elementary school in my home country. It was a "patriotic" poem, meaning an ode to glorify the communist party and its leader. Although I was a good student, it took a long time to learn it by heart. I got up on to the stage in front of my fellow students and teachers, and after delivering a few lines, I froze and couldn't remember a word. I had completely forgotten the poem I had tried so hard to memorize.

I felt ashamed and guilty, not because I couldn't remember the poem or because I was shy, but because the words I was being forced to say sounded so ridiculous and fake. I didn't believe in them and realized that they made absolutely no sense to me. They were just strange sounds, and I was parroting empty words someone had put in my mouth. I felt as if I were speaking an incoherent foreign language.

What is more, all of a sudden the words of the poem had ceased to be words. Instead, they were like air bubbles, frames with no pictures inside. At that time I didn't know anything about *actes manqués*, the refusal to accept one's words unconditionally if one's conscious mind judges them wrong, or doesn't trust their content. I hadn't read Freud and had no explanation for my failure to recite that poem.

Puzzled and helpless, I stared at the other students. Some were laughing, so the teacher tried to comfort me. When I told him that I would never ever agree to recite stupid political poems again, there was a sudden change of tone, and he whispered in my ear, "Watch your words! Beware of what you're saying." This was my first attempt at dissent.

We lived under one of the toughest dictatorships, were watched by the secret police, and were completely isolated from the rest of the world. All that we could do was to try to survive within a closed society and struggle to find our own ways to cope with our political system's obscurantism. One way was to get together in groups selected on the basis of affinities — art, literature, philosophy, or simply a few common tastes.

I remember my parents telling me, "Wherever you go and whatever you do, be aware of words," meaning, "Watch what you're saying." To speak loudly and straightforwardly was dangerous in the communist era. There was irony in the fact that although the dictatorship controlled every aspect of society, the rulers were afraid of our real thoughts and words — the only weapons we could use against them. Political censorship was harsh, and the authorities forever watchful, keeping every form of communication under control.

This lack of freedom is almost impossible for people to understand if they have never lived it. Imagine a world of birdcages, and all the birds, no matter how different from one another, sing the same song *ad infinitum*; in the end, it sounds like a sorrowfully barking dog.

The worst restriction involved freedom of speech. We all knew that if we criticized the communist party or its leaders, we could end up in jail. We weren't supposed to complain about our miserable life, either, or about the nonsense surrounding us. There were spies everywhere, even at our artistic gatherings and inside our literary groups. The restaurants, hotels, or cabins in the mountains were equipped with hidden microphones; our phone lines were tapped.

Communist ideology was based on political slogans and propaganda, on lies and megalomaniacal statements. Language had become distorted. It wasn't only the mass media, harnessed by the powers that be, that was part of the national manipulation; it was also poetry and literature — the arts in general. The country's history was rewritten by authors who had compromised their integrity by slavishly attaching themselves to the political system of the day. In this way, a huge fake mechanism, built on corrupted words, was put in place.

At the time, almost all of us thought communism was there to stay, at least for the duration of our lifetimes. The only way to get used to one's cage was to conjure a parallel world that would save the soul. In addition to the official language, based on fear, caution, and imposed slogans, a parallel language had to be developed — a language that sprang from one's inner sense of freedom, truth, and fairness. Living within this inner world ensured survival — through dissent and a refusal to accept alienation — by sticking to the salvation that came through *real* words and uninhibited communication.

The communist language, based on a utopian form of nationalism, had very specific aims: hiding the truth and manipulating the masses. Eventually, communism collapsed because it had been founded on a false and artificial structure of empty words. The boomerang effect destroyed the mechanism. Still, the damage wrought by a manipulative ideology will persist for decades to come. Corrupt words corrupt mentalities, and the former communist countries will have to struggle with this legacy even longer than it will take them to overcome their economic difficulties.

Words can brainwash one's mind. Think of Hitler's speeches.

Words can be dangerous weapons when used for the purpose of manipulation by evil minds. Fascism is the most tragic example of how a racist and extremist ideology can lead to unspeakable crimes. Words can alter mental structures and influence the collective subconscious. One needs to be aware of their power, watchful of their ambiguities and duplicities, and know that they can cause much harm, both to the individual and to the masses in general. A word planted in your subconscious mind acts like an alien entity. There are theories of *epidemic communication*, linguistic viruses that are spread from person to person. In the long run, the meaning of a word can be amplified or distorted or lose its original meaning.

After the fall of communism, I traveled to different countries and discovered that in addition to ideological manipulations, there are many other types of brainwashing, even in the free world: phony Messiahs propagating religious ideas, proselytizing to the masses to form sects; fake healers selling illusions to crowds and fascinating them with idealistic, pie-in-the-sky promises; a whole industry of advertising bent on exploiting the consumer's oversized expectations.

A slave to high-tech communication, the image swallows the word. We live in a time of ease and comfort. All we have to do is flip a switch, touch a key, dial a number, or plug in this or that device... and we can have everything we desire, from goods and services to information. "Press now for additional happiness" could be the next step of the digital dialogue we have with the institutions and machines that have been created in our "best interests."

Life has improved dramatically from a technical point of view, but what has happened to our soul? Have we found better security, a more balanced way of life? Are we less stressed and more self-confident? Do we communicate better?

America is completely different from the country in which I grew up. People came here and brought along the most advanced technological and artistic achievements: they had dreams to fulfill and found fertile ground for them. They weren't confronted with dictatorships and weren't forced to imagine a parallel life in order to survive. Still, today's America has its forms of alienation. More and more people have the feeling that something is missing in their lives or at least that things are different, and not in a good way, than they were before. The legendary American dream needs to be updated and adapted to new realities and challenges.

My childhood and youth were spent in a communist country where people were condemned to poverty and darkness. Our lives were miserable. We didn't care about cholesterol, pollution, or the negative effects of smoking, nor did we worry about the dangers of obesity, drug addiction, or violence. Many of us managed to preserve our sanity. Our lives were simple. We didn't need antidepressants, although we had good reasons for Prozac. No one sought psychoanalysis, therapists, or other shrinks, although we had good reasons to be clinically depressed.

In a cave, when you have few choices, all sorts of self-defense mechanisms spring into action. One is interpersonal communication. In a primitive society, communication involved ingenuity and directness. We expressed ourselves at times in ways that others might have seen as rude. People talked loudly, gesticulated profusely, and cursed; they lived and hated passionately, were given to making grandiose plans in the evening over many glasses of wine, only to discard them as impossible the next morning. And yet these people were *authentic* in their despair and passionate in their fantasies. They *did communicate!* In the streets, in bars, at gatherings, they kept talking, aware of the words, with secret police watching. They were anything but alienated. Salvation for the soul came from *real* words and freed emotions.

People learned not to trust the official language in the press, in the schools, and at work. Naturally, slavish servants of the regime existed, but most people doubted any political speech and cultivated disbelief and irony as part of their self-defense mechanism. Everybody was aware of living in a "make-believe" world, fully aware of the duplicity of words. Trying to escape from the official language of manipulation, most people quickly learned that they had to think for themselves if they didn't want to be swallowed up by the regime; they had to know what to believe in and what to reject. They had a common enemy — the dictatorship — and thus they had to summon up all their strength to defend the real meanings and consistency of words. They had to be aware of what they were saying and what they were hearing. On one hand, their words could put their lives in danger, and on the other hand, official speech could corrupt their minds.

I have recalled this to emphasize a sensitive issue in our society: today the existence of other forms of manipulation, different from the ones we had to face under communism, yet posing lethal effects, since people's self-defense mechanisms seem to be quite weak here. Having lived their lives in a free world, far from all the complicated issues I've discussed above, they're used to taking each word as true. They've let their guard down; they don't have official enemies within the culture, yet.

A whole industry of advertising, sophisticated commercials, entertainment, and world news is eager to guide, inform, and help.

People don't even have to think much. There are professionals, well paid, who think for them and give them the right answers. They will tell them what to buy, what to eat, when to laugh at sitcoms, how to be happy, successful, and immortal. All they have to do is sit back and enjoy. People here are confident in their values and have no reason to doubt, as long as everything pouring from the TV screens and through all the other communication devices is in their best interest. They think they don't need to be aware of words. They take them for granted. And yet another form of manipulation is at play here, more subtle, in spite of its alleged good intentions. Why resist or oppose it, if it makes things smoother and easier?

Political correctness brings not only social sanity but duplicity; these last years more and more people have felt lonely and confused seeing how their once strong values seem to be fading away. The soul is left aside, while there seems to be, more than ever, a pressure to keep up with the social mechanism and to preserve one's place within it.

Is this depersonalization of the individual the price we have to pay for prosperity in this money-oriented, consumer culture? Is this the consequence of globalization? Maybe it's the result of a "correct" manipulation? I wouldn't bet on it.

ALIENATION THROUGH LANGUAGE

As children, without any electronic or digital excitement to fill (or empty!) our time, we played with words. The only technological entertainment in Romania in the 1960s was Russian black-and-white TV that our parents watched, without much enthusiasm, trying to scrutinize their grim future. Our game was called 'the cordless phone' (at that time none of us imagined that one day such phones would exist)., a game like the one called "telephone" that children play here.

We gathered in front of the monotonous blocks of flats, those pathetic socialist housing projects with balconies full of laundry hanging out to dry, and silently formed a line. The child at the head of the line would whisper something into the ear of the person next to him, careful not to be overheard by the others. The next child would pass on the word he heard to the one next to him, and so on. The child at the end of the line would say the word that had reached him, a word that, most of the time, was quite different from the one with which the game began.

We were amused by the transformation words suffered through our mouths and ears, our subconscious minds creating farcical distortions and innovative acoustical associations. Although the object was to retrieve the initial word at the end of the line, our mendacity and confabulation would take over, and we would intentionally change syllables, slightly altering sounds to indulge our creativity. We just wanted to have fun and, perhaps instinctively, change reality, twist it, and make it more spectacular, more mysterious, putting an ordinary word under a stone and then retrieving an unusual one from beneath it, *different* from the one we knew.

Our game appears today to say much about the function of communication, in which keeping a word intact is broken down by the secret wish to be able to say something different, to optimize reality and change it for the better.

Evidently, spoken language has a greater dynamic than the written, reflecting 'current culture.' Rather the path is reversed. Use of the long-lasting solidity and beauty of the *essential* written *word* saves and enriches the spoken one. But the breakdown between spoken and written language, ignoring the context of the wealth of universal literature, philosophy and art, creates *estrangement through speech* and *alienation through words.*

Lack of time, fatigue, and image overload rob people of the patience and desire for reading bulky classics that could fill minds emptied by routine and force them to ask themselves uncomfortable questions or think independently. It is so much easier to pick up an easy read for the subway or a contemporary best-seller with slick writing, sex, romance, adventure, religious parables, mysteries, or pretentious biographies. Those interested in sampling a culture can also find abbreviated editions of massive classical masterpieces, easily accessible on the internet. "War and Peace" reduced to only a few CDs.

For me as a foreigner, it seemed that here intellectual curiosity is satisfied by dry, synthetic information funneled either through mass-media channels or specialized professional media. College and university graduates specialize in ever more narrow fields. The need to perform and compete in their precise specialty leaves them with neither the time nor the mood to become seriously interested in any topic beyond their profession. To keep up with the information load is exhausting. Vocabulary, expression, speech all gravitate around the same rigorous format.

The American educational system produces first-class specialists, but has less sensitivity for what Europeans call 'general culture.' This amplifies professionalism to the detriment of the more flavorful and unconstrained individual character who can satisfy curiosity or passion in different areas without the pressure of performing by any means possible and/or beyond the oppressive inflexibility of marketing that characterizes American society. Diversity and spiritual wealth, fantasy, and imagination are brought to the United States and kept alive, especially through the immigration of young professionals.

The world is shoddier without self-taught people, dilettantes, and bohemians. It is a more solid society from the point of view of efficiency, but it lacks charm, originality, and metaphor to counterbalance the culture of money with its gratuitous spectacles. Precise language is comfortable through predictability and economy but dull and uninteresting because of its conformity.

In my youth in Eastern Europe, we would chat and have philosophical discussions when we could. That didn't earn us any money, but it enriched our souls. Language would follow and sustain our need for freedom and liberation through the word. In fact, we practiced a type of group therapy, unorganized and without clear goals, centered around the major questions of existence, which made us feel authentic, original, and unique.

We usually met in cafés where the future of the world was debated. In the basement of some university we would improvise discussion groups or at someone's home under the pretext of a 'tea' party (equivalent to any form of alcoholic or artistic expression). No topic would intimidate us, not even issues we hardly knew anything about. We were discovering the world through our own creative powers, using our own words. For us imagination and intuition compensated for knowledge and access to information. We were unprofessional thinkers, reinventing the world and exchanging its unconventional expressions for a refreshing language, unmarked by clichés.

This applied only to certain intellectual groups who used language and culture as guidelines for spiritual defiance. Totalitarianism and its official language was full of slogans and nonsense that manipulated vulnerable parts of society. The dictatorship inhibited intercommunication.

In America, if you stop people in the street and shove a microphone at them, they talk without inhibition, answering questions with serenity and candor. This doesn't mean they say something original or risk swimming against the tide of political correctness and codes of behavior. Words come to them easily — standard expressions extensively used in school, on TV, and in every-day relations, expressions that in turn give an impression of excellence in communication.

The strength and unity of America derive from this uniform diversity, a paradox more evident in New York and other large cities on the east and west coasts, where adhering to the same values is pursued under the pretext of preserving cultural identity within the melting pot. In reality, in order to be adopted and transformed into an efficient and valuable product for society, one needs to become like everyone else, with the same types of reactions, uniform language, and restrained originality.

To be 'different' or 'special' — which was our dream under communism — is a hindrance here. It can only isolate you. The best illustration of this phenomenon is seen in immigrant children. Entering an American school, they immediately yearn to be like everyone else. They dress alike, listen to the same music, adopt the common slang, enjoy fast food, play electronic games; they push themselves to accept the new community values in their desire to be accepted and treated as equals by their colleagues. Their parents quickly learn to speed up their adjustment rather than preserve their differences. Even before becoming fluent in English, they develop trite expressions and conventional communication.

To become an American is an option with rules. English is spoken all over the world, but "American" is beyond language; it's a reflex hiding behind a well-defined process. The verb has supremacy, while metaphor is ignored. Speech that excels in clarity is direct, concise, and simple; it operates with logical structures and mechanical connections. The outcome is a triumph, but it lacks brilliance. It is efficient but not spectacular. Rigor eliminates any superfluous cargo. Personal expressions are useless, as are doubts, dilemmas, questioning outside the molds and shapes imposed by the advertising industry or the mass media.

Some literary genres have all but disappeared, the epistolary for example, which has been completely swallowed by the digital and electronic message. Who is going to write letters these days, when, with a simple touch of a key you can save time, money and words? The personal diary has been replaced by the public blog, and intimacy by a form of verbal exhibitionism in which decency and candor are confused with gratuitous expressions. Who is going to send handwritten cards these days, when all you have to do is add your name (and perhaps *love*) under standard greeting-card texts?

Flat and austere language is counterbalanced by visual assault. From the time we get up to the time we go to bed, we are constantly overwhelmed by commercials in a world tattooed with images. We don't have time for books, but all day we read commercial slogans on walls, buildings, shop windows, taxis, buses, phone booths, on show tickets and programs, T-shirts, and billboards, some even hanging from blimps in the sky. The eye is continuously engaged, besieged until all defense against it is exhausted. The ears are plugged with iPOD ear buds. Thoughts are digitalized.

Another reason for alienation through language could be the loss of confidence in personal expression of our own words. Imagination can be misunderstood in a society fueled by uniformity.

Society protects us from failures in originality by creating classes and programs that teach communication skills to fit the profile of companies. Many places offer free classes to new hires with communication problems to help them be uninhibited in public relations, able to work in a team, speak well publicly, present projects and technical talks to an audience of professionals. Communication means dignity, charm, authority to make yourself heard, and ranges from posture, gesture control, choice of wardrobe, to self-control and being a good listener. There is no dearth of manuals to teach one how to behave in an interview, what guidelines are accepted and recognized, how to sell one's self convincingly and select one's language to please those who only want to hear how well motivated one is.

When I first came to America, I was confused by the use of different meanings attached to the word 'writer,' for example, which for me was a clear, unique, unmistakable occupation. Here I discovered that one could be a *creative writer* (one who is good enough to write commercials), *professional writer* (one who is a teacher ready to make corrections on a beginner's manuscript), *freelance writer* (who doesn't have a job, but writes, with little certainty of commercial success), next to *published author* (at last, a writer who actually writes books and gets them published).

The idealist in me was attracted to the *creative writer* category, not knowing that many street corners display free brochures advertising hundreds of courses that, for a fee and after only a few short months, graduate dozens of 'creative writers.' A writer's talent, domestic or imported, is authenticated by a M.A. program that provides a passport to acceptance by groups, groupies, and closed communities affiliated with universities, clubs, and literary journals, agents and editors. Everything is an industry here, based on intermediaries and governed by commercial laws that leave no room for deviation from the educational establishment, itself an economic mechanism.

Right here and now some questions are called for: How much do words represent us? Are they our ally in a crisis? Could we find refuge in language and uncover forms of self-protection in communication? Are our words a reflection of the thinking and of the self? How much dissimulation is needed, how many masks, subliminal implications, and metaphors must we use to put our life into words without exposing our vulnerability, weaknesses, fragility, and fears? What is the power of words in the information era of cyberspace, technology, and globalization?

We oscillate, whether consciously or not, between a fear of words and a desire to escape from them, on the one hand, and an irresistible attraction to master them, on the other. But not every-thing we feel or think can be put into words.

We may find ourselves inside or outside words, actors involved in the effort to utter them, or simply detached spectators following the play and watching for the appropriate moment when we could intervene as saviors or destroyers, enriching the communication, or emptying it of its meaning. Words have this fluid flexibility to trans-form, pervert or ennoble, depending on the educational and spiri-tual level of the speaker, the listener, and the context of the com-munication.

SOUND AND SILENCE

A tendency to turn concepts, phenomena, and abstract notions into images suits children, who create visual pictures in order to understand the meanings of words they don't understand. They exasperate their parents with repeated questions, while in their minds each synonym or explanation gives the new word a more nearly exact contour, and leads to a revealing metaphor, word/image, thought/emotion, something that sets the static thing into motion. Acoustic associations of letters inside words are as important as logical explanations. Children learn to speak by associating words with objects or persons they can see and touch. With references missing, imagination builds descriptive images based on information the brain can process, a short film where the meaning of a word is gathered in the unfolding "story" of that word.

A foreign language can be learned in the same way. It is acquired when its images in the mother tongue overlap those in the foreign language. It is only then that we can claim to "think" in a foreign language. Or, more poetically, dream in it.

Sometimes expressions that are rich and meaningful in the mother tongue may end up shipwrecked on a foreign shore. An idiom is more than its words. It collects and juggles cultural references, myths, and the folk philosophies and the stages of civilizations through which it has passed, all finely tuned by music, accent, and nudgings from the historical context in which it was originally found. Language brings together all the stories of its words, the images, and metaphors in order to create a new world. In a new key

For writers, this process amounts to rebirth in a different "womb of words." The psychological impact of such a profound displacement exceeds any effort to learn a new language. Moreover, while acquiring some skill in the adopted tongue, a writer may still not be able to create in it, lacking access to the intimate nuances of the other tongue, unable to activate the mental ramifications of creation.

Many writers who enter a different culture feel that their identity has been altered. Uprooted, suspicious, and insecure, they invent a territory between cultures where they remain suspended, a sanctuary but also an excuse for their failures on the new shore. That is when a writer feels that his or her strongest ally, language, has been a traitor, falling short of expressing the depths of his or her writer's soul.

Notions about translation and the relationship between writer and translator have been much debated. Literature abounds with remarkable translators who have transmitted sacred texts and ancient manuscripts, world classics, and landmark books, and yet writers and theorists alike continue to obsess over the *traduttore-traditore* (translator-traitor) problem. The essential element in this controversy is metaphor itself, the key needed to decipher the symbols that differentiate one language from another. Language is a mysterious animal, partly mythical, partly alive, and unfathomable. Metaphor will always protect a language's unique qualities, lock up its magic, and lose the key.

However, even if we do not grasp the meaning, we can appreciate the beauty of a manuscript in Sanskrit, and we can feel profound emotion watching a play performed in ancient Greek, even if we do not know the language. The arts have the exquisite ability to reach heights of understanding beyond language. The opposite phenomenon also occurs. A cascade of words in one's own language some-times can be completely ineffective, empty of meaning, communicat-ing nothing.

How many words do we need to make ourselves understood? What is the essence of communication, and what is the role meta-phor plays in its evolution? To communicate means, etymologically, to convey what we can share. This process implies an interaction based on an exchange of information not only at the conscious level, but at the subconscious as well. The final goal of communica-tion, after all, is *change*.

Communication mainly targets the destruction of limits im-posed by space, matter and time, by the separation between beings and phenomena. It tries to modify the reality one knows with the hope of getting beyond in the wish to improve and expand one's life. The quality of communication stems from the capacity of each individual to develop natural gifts and the desire for knowledge.

Today's new forms of communication — quick and efficient — do not assume beauty, profundity, or spiritual liberation as their goals. Everything has a price. Language continually evolves, some-times losing its power to impress or express no matter how sophisti-cated the means of communication. Communications use and abuse technology, cybernetics, and electronics while detouring or exhausting the magical and primordial force of the word. What can we do to give the word breathing space, while capturing its meaning and ineffable qualities?

In human evolution, speech appeared naturally as a need to ful-fill, to reveal the evolution of consciousness. Communication was an ultimate goal. In the beginning, words expressed the reality of human perception showing the way things are. From drawings carved on cave walls to great biblical allegories, from hieroglyphics to cabalistic manuscripts, to Plato's dialogues or the Homeric epics, metaphor continued to gain importance in communication, deepening an inner mystery, protecting it, and passing it on to the following generations.

What is a metaphor? It can be defined as a linguistic form in which a word or a phrase is used to convey a meaning different from the one it usually carries. Metaphor also implies a comparison, a similarity. The word needs time to find its full self, to achieve an ideal weight, an ineffable density, a proper consistency, in order to have its maximum impact. Ideas, mental or spiritual forms of thought, generate the word; once they find their way into the word, they unravel and become powerless. Once they have entered the public domain, they are open to interpretation and distortion, which may still enrich the expression while preserving their originality.

In essence, communication consists of the spoken, living word, but living words can perish. Once uttered, they can be perverted or lose their intensity, not unlike things that lose their strength and glitter once they are removed from their native environment. Great orators vainly assume that the word, whether spoken or written, ends up in the same place, returns to the great book from whence it came. However, the true master reaches an eternity beyond words. When one looks at the Egyptian pyramids, or at the Sphinx dazzling in the mystery of its simplicity, one hears an entire civilization talking, telling its story. The order, the angles, and the wavy lines in a stone are a concise and brilliant language, as profoundly significant as Beethoven's music or Van Gogh's paintings.

A revealing metaphor is born out of the beauty of primary simplicity as an essence of the world and its meanings rather than a display of hidden meanings. *The Song of Songs, The Mahabharata, The Upanishads, The Dead Sea Scrolls, The Tibetan Book of the Dead,* and comparable Egyptian texts are concentrated dialogues with a divinity, metaphorical trips into the primordial spaces that generate existential concepts and laws, steps in guiding the spirit in its drive to perfection. They are fundamental milestones in the evolution of the expression of communication. The history of mankind rests on metaphors. What are religion, philosophy, arts, if not therapeutic metaphors to serve the soul that strives to communicate, understand, and be understood?

A word is itself a metaphor, merging the imaginary with the real, marking limits and superimposing abstractions on the material. But metaphor can wrap itself around the word, with all its fleshy layers, with its light and shadowy undulations, with well-chosen sounds and significant silences, creating a unique cosmic body through the revelation of birth as a result of the initial *naming.*

God used Man as a metaphor of genius to explore the limits of His *own* creation. He multiplied through us into *words* and left us free to try forever to decode the metaphor of His creation. Some take it as a gift, others as a curse; some perceive it as a burden, others as a privilege.

Theologians discuss God, employing metaphors that humanize Him and thus challenge His presumably boundless limits. God controls lives without any promises or certainties, with no proof of an afterlife. However, this authoritarian relationship between the Creator and His creation can be broken down through the intervention of the miraculous, the metaphors with which we measure our existence, like Magellans scrutinizing earth from the horizon.

WORDS ARE TIME

In a temporal and magical way, words are associated with the Beginning in all ancient cultures and myths. In Egyptian writings, for example, the god Thoth, the inventor of hieroglyphs as symbols of the divine discourse, *creates the world by uttering it*. He names the divisions of time and space, and they come into being. He names the elements, the laws, the movement of all things, gives names to life forms. According to *The Egyptian Book of the Dead*, Thoth is the god of the *power of words*, of the creating verb, of magic and the mystery of mummification. Thoth was also recognized by the ancient Greeks, who deemed him to be like their own god, Hermes.

The Christian gospel also refers to the creation of the world through the word of grace: the Gospel according to John affirms that "*In the beginning was the Word.*" A parallel can be found in the Hindu *Upanishads,* which describe the birth of the universe out of primordial sound, the human voice of the Eternal Principle. The sacred book *Popul Vuh* of the Quiche Maya civilization recounts *The Beginning as immobility and silence in the dark, in the night... and then came the Word.* The omnipotent Word appears many times in the Old Testament, for in the Hebraic tradition, the creation of the world begins with the spiritual motivations behind the language.

If in the beginning there was the Word, splitting light from dark, unifying body and spirit, in the end what matters is its direction and journey. We are given to words as much as they are given to us. On this two-way street one can travel imaginary or unimaginable distances from essence to discovery while being the slave and the master of words, alternately acting as explorer, magician, adven-

159

turer, or builder.

In the oldest civilizations and cultures of Egypt, India, Tibet, Central America, Africa and Japan, one finds that language was passed on as a meaningful dowry, or that it conveys secret power. When people chant magic words, prayers, hymns and religious rituals, suggestions and hypnotic trances or magic rituals, *certain words* carry forces capable of producing natural or supernatural transformations, of unveiling mysteries and attracting miracles. A loud intonation or murmur broken by breathing and pauses, repetition carrying a certain musicality of specific sounds and potent words in the verbal formulae of mantras, incantations, and invocations is assumed to free latent powers that were used to reach certain goals by prophets, apostles, mystics, priests, shamans, healers, spiritual leaders, and magicians of all sorts.

The Egyptians imagined words as concrete objects. If words, considered objects of personal strength, had been stolen from a person, that person would become vulnerable, exposed to illnesses, to any aggressive or abusive act. In modern times, the fear of losing one's powerful words is equivalent to alienation arising from losing the profound and intimate meaning of communication.

For the ancients, words were magic entities capable of predicting the future and changing reality. Their relationship to their gods, the inexplicable, and death as a prelude to the afterlife, was refined by significant sounds and phrasings. Words were thought to carry great energy and were capable of sending the divinity messages through which the primordial order could be changed. The name was also a magical entity, keeping its power even beyond the death of the person who carried it.

Almost all cultures believe in the sacredness of the words that come from the Creator. Today's disregard for words therefore could be regarded as an estrangement from God. In standardizing communication, we lose the sacredness of words, alienating us from the divinity.

The Creator protects its mystery. The sacred writings synthesize simple teachings: rise above the word and you will become essence, or, losing control, you will go mad. Dive into it and you will understand. You hide inside words, and through them you also let yourself be revealed. Communication is the game with which we throw each other words, like balls in the air that can send us sky high or knock us for a loop.

෨

If we believe that life on earth is a divine metaphor, then *spirit is the metaphor of the body carrying it.* The history of mankind, therefore, becomes a seductive allegory. Its metaphysics could deliver us even from the fear of death, implicitly a metaphor itself.

We have an inborn predisposition to accept the metaphoric, rather than the direct meaning, especially when it comes to painful topics. While we refuse to accept death, we are ready to embrace the ideas of rebirth, of paradise, an eternal journey through the universe awaiting reincarnation, or we wish to be as close as possible to the gate though which the Messiah will pass. While we do not trust our spiritual powers, we feel a connection to the guardian angels in Renaissance frescos. We are more afraid of the hell after death than of the one around us. We protect our emotions, and we ignore the naked truth.

Metaphors are the most sensitive barometers for registering the evolution of communication. Standardization, meaningless clichés, globalization, and depersonalization are signs of the alienation from language itself. Metaphors dry out. The remains are empty, hollow, tasteless, perhaps even poisonous.

As children we were fascinated by tales where reality was recreated in a way that allowed us to touch boundaries out of human reach.

Legends, mythology and stories are our first encounter with fantastic literature where everything is possible. They resemble dreams projecting us into other dimensions, where miracles are accepted without question. How it is possible to fly, to cross forbidden boundaries, to meet one who is dead, to possess supernatural powers? Metaphors make childhood happy. Stories are read at bedtime because their symbolic universes offers safety and a soothing refuge.

The instinctive escape from reality starts in childhood and grows deeper with age. Only later does the metaphor lose its grandeur — namely when our rapport with the world changes. We are no longer willing to make room for symbols among the conglomeration of small concrete facts destroying our reality.

Overwhelmed by responsibilities, tired and stressed, grilled by daily routine, tense, or simply bored, most of us are no longer able to recognize the *existential metaphor* itself. Rather than living the metaphor, we study it in specialized environments. It turns into a linguistic whim, or it can be faulted for its "unrealistic" side, distracting people from the daily "reality," which has to be dealt with in an alert and competitive society, one in need of soldiers and not dreamers.

American art and literature offer examples of the sublimation of metaphor in favor of the direct expression of a minimalist universe, of daily life made up of gestures, incidents, and feelings arranged in simple artistic forms, not without humor or irony.

In communist Romania, where I spent my formative years as a writer, the metaphor was our principal weapon to evade political censorship, a twisted but successful way to see one's books published. Although biographies and memoirs were almost impossible to squeeze through the tight net of censorship, poetry and prose could be enveloped in a protective shell of metaphor and allegory tough enough to get the forbidden truth out regardless of whether it was about political or social reality.

Latin American writers experienced the same situation in their totalitarian societies. Novels like Marquez's *A Hundred Years of Solitude* and *The Autumn of the Patriarch* are fantastic allegories hiding inexorable social aspects of a time when historians were silenced, leaving the writers — who were equipped with metaphor — to carry out the task of witnessing an absurd and traumatizing world.

It was the same with Soviet literature. Writing between the lines and using allusions soon turned an exhausting exercise into an art, a "style" now imposed as an artistic formula.

Once I had arrived in America, I discovered that the metaphor had often been destroyed willingly. Nobody needed it. Nobody missed it. Moreover, people considered it a carrier of disguised truths, either deploring its entanglements, or refusing to make sense of it. It took me some time to accept this in my own writing. I am not sure where I am today, oscillating between two worlds, juggling verbs and imagination, in an attempt to reconcile the two hemispheres

Another category is the *political metaphor* used in the official discourse to manipulate, to transform perceptions of uncomfortable decisions, to offer palliatives for austere and unsatisfying realities. There is also the *commercial metaphor*, through which reality is adjusted and illusions are optimized in symbols to meet ideals of the masses. Often, commercials use the *speculative metaphor* to convince us to buy a product. Ideologies also manipulate psychologically speculative metaphors to command attention or to seduce the audience.

The strongest of all is the *religious metaphor*; even more powerful than the *artistic*, which may be the one best entitled to define the absolute. However, since persistence and widespread influence tend to legitimize rules, definitions, and laws, the religious metaphor, with its unexpected current impact and consequences, reigns supreme. Civilizations rise and fall under its sign: wars and conflicts begin; myths and heroes — authentic, fake, or invented — have been created. In its name, nations were saved, people were manipulated, and people have been killed.

Communism misappropriated metaphors. It identified *the soul* as the main enemy and denied any faith that was outside its utopia. Demolishing churches and synagogues was not enough. That merely eliminated places of worship, but they also got to destroy the *metaphors of spirituality*, in the attempt to make people appear weak and vulnerable, humiliating them.

Luckily, the experiment failed in Eastern Europe. The majority recreated the *metaphor of resistance* in their own homes; they carried it in their souls and imagined personal forms of self-protection, took refuge in culture, humor, carelessness, and frivolity. In the absence of freedom of expression, truths are encoded. People find their refuge in metaphors. Dictatorships split the personalities of individuals, forcing them to encode communication and develop parallel worlds where each is searching for metaphors along with a mechanism for personal survival.

In America we are spared these acrobatics of daily life and language. We live in a free world, accustomed to democracy. But this doesn't mean that we are shielded from fear or that a free market society doesn't encourage other kinds of alienation. Even freedom produces anxiety, uncertainty, fear of failure, of loneliness, of the future, of death. These feelings may be amplified, as the world we live in is one more complex, tough, selective, and unforgiving to those who do not measure up to the competitive mechanism. Once thrown into a free society's mixer, the soul is in need of saving metaphors that can measure up to the needs of the culture.

Soon after moving to New York I discovered a well-defined system of intermediaries and mediators that operates between the individual and authority. I came from a world where we faced necessities on our own, continuously fighting rigidity, obtuseness, and institutional bureaucracy. We were accustomed never to prevailing against authority, inside a legislative system both fragile and corrupt, with limited rights. The only freedom left was the chance to fight alone against the windmills of an enclosed and arrogant society.

Over here, any step one takes needs "assistance." One should go through lawyers, managers, brokers, agents for anything and everything. They negotiate and mediate the dialogue between the individual and the institution. In spite of protections and all the modern conveniences offered by this well-regulated system, the soul has its own troubles. While society is efficient, therapists proliferate.

Alienation and depression are no joke. More and more elementary school students see therapists. Later the picture may be complicated by psychiatric issues, rising out of drug abuse, peer pressure, or unstable family life. Careers bring anxiety, insomnia, depression, fear of the future.

At some point I thought that everybody I had met in New York had a personal therapist. The city seemed to have an equal number of patients and shrinks. Never would I have thought that the successful, self-confident men I met at various events had their weekly therapy sessions, or that the elegant ladies, poised and carefree, would return on Mondays from their vacation homes in order not to miss theirs. Perhaps it is a way to socialize, I thought to myself, or a fashion.... Many of my friends were on daily sleeping pills and antidepressants. I confess that I suspected many of them of snobbery or boredom. However, time proved my suspicions wrong; I understood the pressure, stress, alienation, and unhappiness troubling a world that had grandly planned for everything but its victims.

In this country, we are distanced from ourselves, alienated from our own healing powers, forced to deplete our energies in a relentless dynamic, itself governed by the increasingly accelerated rhythm of the world. Even time seems to have run away from us, and each year rushes toward something more uncertain.

There is always profit in treating our fears or discussing our loneliness. The system isn't going to pay attention to us for free, and the competitive mechanism operates through exact rules, governed by political correctness, commercial laws, and social pragmatics. True salvation can come for each only from the inside.

However, being your own healer through your own words is not a subject taught in school. It cannot be found in textbooks and is not endorsed by any court. Salvation through words is a personal discovery, so fascinating in itself it could be a "therapy for life."

THE HOROSCOPE OF LANGUAGE

According to *Genesis*, when only one language was spoken on earth, people planned to build a tower, called Babel, high enough to reach Heaven. (The word Babel derives from the Hebrew word *balal*, which means *to mix, to confound*.) This provoked God's anger, and He saw it as an affront. He came down to earth to confront the offenders and punish them for their audacity in thinking they could ascend to Heaven. God mixed up their language so that they could no longer understand each other. He divided them into dialects and races spread around the globe. In losing their unified language, people lost the chance to climb to Heaven as well.

Beyond the biblical story, there are sufficient reasons to believe that all languages have a common source or that key sonorities with similar meanings exist in different languages. This theory was developed by a master of occult sciences, Rudolf Steiner, who founded the Anthroposophy Society in 1912 and authored numerous studies analyzing the biblical mystery of *Genesis* and propounding its scientific, religious, and spiritual interpretations.

In his work *Speech and Drama*, Steiner introduces the idea of "visible discourse" as a harmony between sound and movement, and also the idea of a universal language based on the value of significant sounds common to all languages. For Steiner and for cabalist erudites, language is not mainly for communication but for *creation*. The uttering of each letter is a complex act of creation, while the word is an entity describing a material form in the air, capable of transforming abstract concepts into sensory images. A word is *seen* initially and only understood later. Its intonation stimulates a strong image capable of resonating and vibrating on the same note as the universal order.

According to Steiner, the letters of the alphabet spoken in a certain way can generate an ethereal body in which the consonants reflect "exterior happenings" while vowels represent "interior experience." The letter H, placed in the middle of the road between consonants and vowels, is associated with breathing. According to Steiner's theory, each spoken word creates a stimulus capable of influencing our destiny. He considered Hebrew to be the original language, the universal basis from which dialects are derived, and the spiritual bridge connecting all languages.

Israeli Yehuda Tagar, Steiner's disciple, unraveling the similarities between languages, goes further, identifying a hidden power in language, in acoustic patterns capable of inducing behavioral or mental modifications. He developed a new method, "Philophonetica," (which can be translated as "love of sounds" or "the soul in relationship with the sound"), which he recommends not only to acting classes, but also in psychological therapy for the effects certain sounds and words can have on the body-soul unity. Music has been shown to have a healing role. Major tonality is considered reinvigorating, while a minor key has a soothing or passive effect.

Targar endows letters as sounds with attitudes, moods, and actions finely tuned to the inflection of words, tones, and musicality. Essentially, his theory maintains that certain similarities in languages are due to the fact that similar experiences are expressed through similar sounds.

The theory is fascinating in part because of the examples he gives showing a correlation between cosmic and elementary dimensions of letters as synthesizing sounds. Each consonant corresponds to a constellation. Each vowel, depending on the pronunciation, claims a planet, the sun, or the moon. Behind each letter of the alphabet, there is an element of nature. As a whole, sounds make up "the language of life," reuniting all kinds of experiences — physical, psychological, and spiritual — generating congruent or antagonistic energies inside the words.

Words can be catalogued in a *horoscope of language,* as *words of water, air, fire,* and *earth.* Words can float in front of our eyes hypnotically, like fish in an aquarium. Some can drift along separated from their shells. We can imagine them penetrating stone and burning down appearances, just as they can also plunge inside the core of things, digging into their essence; they will remain silently there, in a conspiracy with time, awaiting their moment of liberation, freeing their intact energies. In their absence, chaos and darkness will reign. In a biblical norm, what are words if not *light?*

Words of water, "*water words,*" are proper to the fluidity of language, the suppleness and flexibility of communication. They belong to those who have an ease of expression and presence of mind and who are uninhibited in using language. They are characteristic of orators and clowns, of intelligent and inventive minds, of actors and gossips. Lucky the linguistic emigrant who is able to carry his words of water to the other language, heavy with memories! The language of water is natural; it takes the shape of the place it inhabits and flows easily, serving the personality of the speaker. It borrows from other languages, easily adapting to any situation. It is permissive and disposed to divagations.

Words of air, "*air words,*" are transparent essence. They are much like drops of fine perfume on a delicate wrist, like a breath of grace, or the most intimate thought rarefied like the wing of an angel descending from the divine. They float easily inside the language of arts and philosophy, carrying the weight of the world like a feather. Producers of catharsis, concentrating emotions in linguistic molecules, air words have a direct connection to the muse of inspiration. The language of air gives unlimited credit to metaphors; at the same time it encourages the speaker to climb spiritual steps.

Words of fire, "*fire words,*" express energetic personalities, revolutionary spirits, remarkable adventurers, or opinion makers. They give a speaker the strength to preach, even in vain, animated by often impossible missions and unattainable ideals. *Fire* is the language of leadership and action, able to determine big changes and to challenge limits.

The words of earth, "*earth words,*" express personalities who are "down to earth." They tend to associate with the positive. Their language is cold, direct, and exact; their thinking is lucid but cautious and logical. As people they are shy, equivocal, linguistically refined.

Intonation, inflection, gesture, and facial expression, as well as musicality can enrich communication with force and credibility. In this dynamic and creative process, language shapes itself around the temperament and personality of the speaker, supporting the most intimate thoughts, protecting emotions and vulnerability. It becomes his *ally* and serves his ego.

The expressions and forms of communication are unlimited, but how many really enter our consciousness? How many do we credit and use during this life?

We are left with metaphor to enable us to explore what is otherwise inaccessible. The revealing or saving metaphor both enlightens and calms.

ABOUT THE AUTHOR

Carmen Firan, born in Romania, is a poet, fiction writer, and playwright. She has published in her native country twenty books of poetry, novels, essays and short stories. She is also the author of several plays and film scripts. Since 2000, she has been living in New York. Her writings have appeared in translation in many literary magazines and in various anthologies in France, Israel, Sweden, Germany, Ireland, Poland, Canada, Britain, and the United States. She is a member of the PEN American Center and The Poetry Society of America. She has translated several American writers into Romanian. See her website: www.carmenfiran.com

༛

"The secret of how the deeply farcical and the profoundly human can coexist and engender one another has been patented by Eastern European writers. Carmen Firan's stories are heirs to that tradition, and the world of her stories is filled with the pathos of people caught by uniquely contemporary dilemmas. These are stories of exile, loss, history, love, and just plain surprise at the oddness of being human at this time. Poetry and humor infuse her world, and the chill of strange magic is always in the air...An exciting view of life, love, and the meaning of existence, through the eyes of a renowned East European writer... Carmen in New York, like Lorca in New York, is both tonic & necessary." —Andrei Codrescu, author of *Wakefield*, NPR commentator

༛

"Poet, writer, essayist, Carmen Firan is blessed with an open, complementary personality, not a closed one. In an outstanding, original way, this author knows how to endow ideas with concreteness and give an aura of imagination to realist observations. Though in this book her poems are missing, POETRY breathes throughout, even in its erudite passages. Carmen Firan demonstrates in its two reciprocative sections, that there are no bodiless ideas or fleshless words. This, finally, calls itself Talent and Creativity. —Nina Cassian, author of *Take My Word for It*

❧

"Carmen Firan is a crafter of wickedly satirical, sly, and subtle short fictions that continually surprise the delighted reader, while illuminating some of life's crazier and more poignant perspectives.... Her subtle yet vividly intense writings of the artist's inner life range from Bucharest and New York to invented submarine and subterranean landscapes of mind. Mixed in her bitter memory of an oppressive totalitarian society is her sparkling ironic wit." —Isaiah Sheffer, artistic director of Symphony Space and host of NPR series, *Selected Shorts*

❧

"Who is Carmen Firan? A voice broken by exile like glass shattered against a rock. But all these pretty shards, in the naked light, said something, too, to this woman who can't leave language alone; and patiently she gathered them, risking the cuts, to fashion a new, fractured voice for a New World.... She kept speaking and kept writing, and thus brought us the gift of her wonderful words that became the swirling pages of this wonderful book....

"It took a survivor of Eastern European tyranny like Carmen Firan to reveal the true absurdity of the American story. What seems